Instructor's Manual

THE MACMILLAN READER

Judith Nadell
Glassboro State College

John Langan
Atlantic Community College

Linda McMenamin
Glassboro State College

Macmillan Publishing Company
New York

Macmillan Publishing Company
866 Third Avenue, New York, New York 10022

Collier Macmillan Canada, Inc.

Printing: 3 4 5 6 7   Year: 8 9 0 1 2 3

ISBN 0-02-386020-0

CONTENTS

TEACHING COMPOSITION WITH THE MACMILLAN READER

One of the pleasures of teaching is getting together informally with colleagues to trade ideas, air problems, share light moments, and speculate about why some assignments set off fireworks while others quickly fizzle out.

In this Instructor's Manual, we would like to share with you some thoughts about teaching freshman composition and talk about ways of using THE MACMILLAN READER. We'll explain our approach for introducing each rhetorical pattern and indicate what we emphasize when discussing the professional essays in each section. Also, we'll suggest possible answers to the "Questions for Close Reading" and "Questions about the Writer's Craft" that follow each professional essay. We want to emphasize, though, that our responses are not meant to be definitive. Although we purposely avoided open-ended, anything-goes questions, you should keep in mind that our responses represent our view only. You may not agree with all our interpretations. That's fine. If nothing else, our answers may suggest another way of viewing an essay.

At the Start of the Course

Frankly, many students dread freshman composition-- a hard pill to swallow for those of us who have made the teaching of writing our life's work. But it's important to understand that many students' past experiences with writing have not been positive. Rather than trying to pretend that all our students are pleased about being in a writing class, we work to get out in the open any unhappiness they may have about writing and writing teachers.

Here's how we go about airing any negative feelings that may exist. On the first day of class, we acknowledge students' feelings by saying something like this: "I imagine some of you wish you didn't have to take this course. In fact, you may feel that the only thing worse would be having to take a course in public speaking." Our remark elicits smiles of self-recognition from many students, and the whole class seems to relax a bit. Then we ask students to explain why they approach the writing course with such uneasy feelings. Many have horror stories to tell, sad tales about writing courses and writing teachers. Here are summaries of some of the comments we've heard over the years.

. In the past, my papers were returned so covered with red ink that I could barely make out my own writing. I felt discouraged to see how much I had done wrong and angry to see my work covered over with comments.

. I could never figure out what my teachers wanted. Different teachers seemed to look for different things. Since there were no clear standards, I've never understood the qualities that make up good writing.

. Writing papers always took me too much time and felt like an endless chore. Getting a first draft done was hard enough, but revising was even worse. And the payoff for writing several drafts didn't seem worth the effort.

- I knew in my head what I wanted to say but didn't know how to get my thoughts down on paper. My ideas never came out quite right.

- I had writer's block whenever I sat down to put pen to paper. I stared at the desk, daydreamed, fidgeted, and had real trouble getting started. Finally, just before an assignment was due, I dashed off something to hand in, just to get it over with.

As such sentiments are aired, students discover that their experience has not been unique; they learn that others in class have had similarly frustrating experiences. We also confirm students' impressions by telling them that each semester many students recount comparable sagas of woe. We reassure the class that we understand the obstacles, both inner and outer, they have to face when writing. And we tell them that we will work to make the freshman writing course as positive an experience as possible. But we also say that we'd be dishonest if we led them to believe that writing is easy. It isn't. We have no magic formula for turning them into A-plus writers. On the other hand, because we are writers and because we work with writers, we know that the composing process can be satisfying and rewarding. We tell the class that we hope they'll come to share our feelings as the semester progresses.

From here, we move to an activity which continues to break the ice while also familiarizing the class with the workshop format we use at various points in the semester. Students form groups of two and then four, chatting with each other for about five minutes each time. To get them moving, we put some questions on the board: what are their names, where are they from, where are they living while attending college, what other courses are they taking, what is their intended major, and so on. After a few seconds of nervous silence, the class begins to buzz with friendly energy.

When ten minutes or so have passed, we stop the activity and explain why we "wasted" precious class time just socializing. During the semester, we explain, they will learn a good deal about writing from other classmates as they meet in small groups and respond to each other's work. So it makes sense for them to get to know each other a bit right at the outset. Also, we tell the class that we hope they will find sharing their writing as interesting and fun as chatting together. As a final step in building a spirit of community, we circulate a piece of paper on which each student writes his or her name and phone number. Before the next class, we have the sheet typed and reproduced so that everyone can have a copy of the class directory.

Assigning the First Two Chapters in the Book

During the first or second class, we emphasize to students that the course should help them become sharper readers as well as stronger writers. With that in mind, we assign the chapter on "The Reading Process" as well as the chapter on "The Writing Process," up to the section titled "Organizing the Evidence" (page 33). While the writing chapter may be assigned all at once, we've found that it works more effectively when broken into two assignments. Since the writing process is at the heart of the course, we want to make sure students read the chapter carefully enough to understand the process fully.

When students return to class having read the reading chapter and the first part of the writing chapter, we answer any questions they may have and go over the answers for the activities in the writing chapter (see page 11 of this manual). Then we move into a discussion of prewriting. We tell the class that prewriting loosens a writer up. Exploratory and tentative, prewriting helps reduce the anxiety many people feel when facing the blank page. With prewriting, a writer doesn't have to worry, "This better be good." After all, no one except the writer is going to read the prewritten material.

The best way for students to discover what prewriting is like is for them to try it for themselves. So, we say, "Let's suppose you had to write an essay on why students dislike English classes or what teachers could do to make English courses more interesting." Then we ask them to select one prewriting technique discussed in the book (questioning the subject, brainstorming, freewriting, or mapping) to generate the raw material for such an essay. Often, we distribute scrap paper or yellow lined paper for them to use, reinforcing the message that prewriting is tentative and vastly different from finished work.

At the end of the class, we ask students to use the prewriting just prepared in class as the basis for the first draft of an essay. And we assign the rest of the writing chapter, telling students to pay special attention to the guidelines in the chapter, especailly those in the sections "Organizing the Evidence" and "Writing and Connecting the Parts of the Essay."

At the start of the next class, we review the rest of the writing chapter and discuss the answers to the chapter's activities. We've found that many students do not understand that writing is a process. Having them go through the sequence described in the chapter introduces them to the concept of process and shows them what one process might be like. And now that they have had a taste of the writing process, it is time to explain (as the book does on pages 14 and 51-52) that each writer customizes the steps in the sequence to suit his or her needs and style. Not everyone writes the same way, we emphasize, and we urge students to choose the approach that works best for them.

Students then take out the first draft of their papers. But we do not have them hand in the essays. Instead, we have them get back into the same groups of two they were in the previous class and spend about ten minutes giving each other feedback on the effectiveness of the drafts. To focus their observations, they are asked to use the checklist on page 51. After hearing their partner's response to their work, students get busy revising their essay right there in class. We then collect the papers, promising only to read--not grade--them. Reviewing the papers, we explain, will give us a good sense of what each writer does well and what needs to be worked on. Finally, we end the class by telling students that we don't expect them to have mastered all the material in the book's first two chapters. But now that they have read the chapters carefully and have worked through the reading and writing processes, they should have a clear sense of how to proceed during the rest of the semester. We assure them that throughout the course we will refer to the opening two chapters as need arises.

Ways to Use the Book

THE MACMILLAN READER is arranged according to nine rhetorical modes: description, narration, exemplification, process analysis, comparison-contrast, cause-effect, definition, division-classification, and argumentation-persuasion. The more accessible experiential modes are presented first, before moving on to the more demanding analytic patterns.

If you prefer to design the course around themes rather than rhetorical patterns, the thematic table of contents will help you select essays on timely issues. In such a course, we recommend that you have students read a number of essays on an issue. The fact that several essays on the same issue use different rhetorical strategies helps students see that the patterns are not ends in themselves, but are techniques that writers use to make their points. And the introductions to the patterns will help students understand the distinctive features of specific rhetorical strategies.

If you adopt a rhetorical approach in the course, you need not feel confined by the order of patterns in the book; each chapter is self-contained, making it possible for you to sequence the modes however you wish. And, of course, there's no need to cover all the essays in a chapter or even all the rhetorical patterns. It is more realistic to assign two or three selections per pattern, perhaps concentrating on one of the selections for class discussion. A word of warning: If you tell a class which of several assigned selections will be discussed, some students will skip the other selections. You'll probably want to explain to students that there are many ways to use a rhetorical pattern and that reading all the assigned essays will give them an understanding of the options available.

In rhetorically-organized courses, we suggest that you emphasize early in the semester that professional writers don't set out to write an essay in a particular mode. The patterns emerge as the writers prewrite and organize their ideas; they come to see that their points can be best made through a particular rhetorical strategy or combination of strategies.

It's helpful, we've learned, to assign selections before and after students write an essay. For example, if students are going to write a causal analysis, you might have them read "The Faltering Family" and "In Other Words." Then, after reviewing their drafts and seeing the problems they have had with, let's say, causal chains, you might have them examine the way Thomas traces complex causal relationships in "The Health Care System."

Some instructors using a rhetorical approach in their courses place a special emphasis on exposition. If this is your orientation, you might want to begin with the exemplification chapter. That section stresses the importance of establishing a clear thesis and providing solid support for the essay's central point. Then you might move to the description and narration chapters; these underscore the importance of, respectively, a dominant impression and a narrative point, both developed through specific supporting details.

Creating a Process-Oriented Class Environment

We've found that creating a workshop atmosphere in the classroom helps students view writing as a process. When a new paper is assigned, we try to give students several minutes to start their prewriting in class. In other classes, time may be set aside for students to rework parts of their first draft. We may, for instance, ask them to sharpen their introductions, conclusions, sentence structure, or transitions.

In our experience, it's been especially productive to use class time for peer evaluations of first drafts. For these feedback sessions, students may be paired with one other classmate or they meet with three or four other classmates. (We've found groups of more than five unwieldy.) Feedback from someone other than the course instructor motivates students to put in more time on a draft. Otherwise, some of them will skip the revision stage altogether; as soon as they've got a draft down on paper, they'll want to hand it in. Hearing from other classmates that a point is not clear or that a paragraph is weakly developed encourages students to see that revision involves more than mechanical tinkering. They start to understand that revision often requires wholesale rethinking and reworking of parts of the essay. And, after a few feedback sessions, students begin to identify for themselves the problem areas in their own writing.

You'll find that many students squirm at the thought of reacting to their classmates' work. So it's not surprising that they tend to respond to each other's papers with either indiscriminate praise or unhelpful neutrality. To guide students, we prepare a brief checklist of points to consider when responding to each other's work. (You might, for example, adapt the checklist on page 51 to fit a particular assignment). With such a checklist in front of them, students are able to focus their impressions and provide constructive feedback.

There are a number of ways to set up peer feedback sessions. Here are a few you may want to use:

. After pairing students or placing them in small groups, have each essay read aloud by someone other than the author. Students tell us that hearing another person read what they've written is invaluable. Awkward or unclear passages in a paper become more obvious when someone who has never before seen the essay reads it aloud.

. Place students in small groups and ask them to circulate their papers so that everyone has a chance to read all the essays. Then have each group select one especially effective paper to read aloud to the rest of the class. Alternately, you may ask each group to select a strong essay that needs work in a few spots. These essays are then read aloud to the rest of the class. Everyone discusses each paper's strengths and what might be done to sharpen the sections that miss the mark.

. Ask one or two students to type their drafts of an assignment on a ditto master. Or they may make enough photocopies so that everyone can look at the papers. In class, the other students--either as a whole or in groups--react to the papers up for scrutiny that day.

A quick aside: At the start of the course, students are reluctant to "offer their papers up for sacrifice"--as one student put it. But once they're accustomed to the process, they are not at all skittish and even volunteer to be "put on the chopping block"--another student's words. They know that the feedback received will be invaluable when the time comes to revise.

As you no doubt can tell, we confess to a real liking for group work. Since it gives students the chance to see how others approach the same assignment, they come to appreciate the personal dimension to writing and develop an awareness of rhetorical options. The group process also multiplies the feedback students obtain for their work, letting them see that their instructor is just one among many readers. Group activities thus help them gain a clearer sense of purpose and audience. Finally, we have found that peer review encourages students to be more active in the classroom. When students assume some of the tasks traditionally associated with the instructor, the whole class becomes more animated and vigorous.

Some Cautions About Group Work

If you are new to group work, you may have the uneasy feeling that the group process can deteriorate into enjoyable but unproductive bull sessions. That can happen if the instructor does not guide the process carefully.

Here are several suggestions to steer you clear of some of the traps that can ensnare group activities. First, we recommend you give very clear instructions about how students are to proceed. Providing a checklist, for example, directs students to specific issues you want them to address. Second, we believe in establishing a clear time schedule for each group activity.

We might say, "Take five minutes to read to yourself the paper written by the person on your left," or "Now that all the papers in your group have been read, you should vote to determine which is the strongest paper. Then take five minutes to identify one section of the essay that needs additional attention." And third, although we try to be as inconspicuous as possible during group work, we let students know that we are available for help when needed. Sometimes we circulate among the groups, listening to comments, asking a question or two. But more often we stay at the desk and encourage students to consult with us when they think our reaction would be helpful.

Responding to Student Work

Beyond the informal, in-class consultations just described, we also meet during the course with each student for several one-on-one conferences of about fifteen to thirty minutes. Depending on our purpose, student needs, class size, and availability of time, a number of things may occur during the individual conferences. We may review an already-graded and commented-upon paper, highlighting the paper's strengths and underscoring what needs to be done to sharpen the essay. Or we might use the conference to return and discuss a recent essay which has or has not been graded. In the last few years, both of us have tended not to grade or write comments on a paper we're going to review in conference. Instead, we take informal notes about the papers and refer to them when meeting with students. We've found that this approach encourages students to interact with us more freely since their attention isn't riveted to the comments and grade already recorded on the paper. Finally, we end each conference by jotting down a brief list of what the student needs to concentrate on when revising or writing the next assignment. Students tell us this individualized checklist lets them know exactly what they should pay attention to in their work.

When students hand in the final draft of a paper, we ask them to include their individualized checklist. Having a checklist for each student enables us to focus on the elements that typically give the student trouble. And, quite candidly, having the checklists in front of us tames our not-so noble impulse to pounce on every problem in an essay.

In our oral and written comments, we try to emphasize what's strong in the essay and limit discussion of problems to the most critical points. Like everyone else, students are apt to overlook what they've done well and latch on to things that haven't been so successful. If every error a student makes is singled out for criticism, the student--again, like everyone else--often feels overwhelmed and defeated. So unless a student is obviously lackadaisical and would profit from some hard-hitting, teacherly rebukes, we try to make our comments as positive and as encouraging as possible. And rather than filling the paper with reworked versions of, let's say, specific sentences and paragraphs, we make liberal use of such remarks as these: "Read these last three sentences aloud. Do you hear the awkwardness? How could you streamline these sentences?" or "Doesn't this paragraph contradict what you say at the beginning of the preceding paragraph? What could you do to eliminate the confusion?"

When responding to a paper, we often suggest that the student review or reread a professional essay, the introduction to a rhetorical pattern, or sections of the writing chapter. And we always end our comments with a brief list of points to be added to the student's personalized checklist.

At the End of the Course

Since our students keep all their papers in a folder, they have no trouble retrieving essays written weeks or even months earlier. So, near the end of the semester, we ask students to select--for one more round of revision--three or four essays, with each paper illustrating a different rhetorical pattern. We use these reworked versions of the essays to assign a final grade to each student. If you structure your course around themes and issues, you'll probably want to require that each paper deal with a different theme.

As the semester draws to a close, we also ask students to complete the questionaire at the back of the book (page 698). Their responses let us know which selections worked well and which did not, helping us make adjustments in future semesters. So that you too can find out how the class reacted to the assigned selections, you might ask students to give the completed forms to you rather than having students mail their questionnaires to the publisher. If you do collect the forms, we hope that you'll forward them to us at Macmillan after you've had a chance to look them over. This kind of student feedback will be crucial when we revise the book.

An especially rewarding way to end the semester is to have the class publish a booklet of student writing. Students revise and then submit two of their strongest papers to a class-elected editorial board which selects one essay from each student in the class, being sure that the essays chosen represent a mix of styles and rhetorical approaches. After a table of contents and a cover are prepared, the essays are retyped, duplicated, and stapled into booklet form. Depending on the equipment and funds available, the booklet may be mimeographed, dittoed, or photocopied.

Students respond enthusiastically to this project. After all, who can resist the prospect of being published? And knowing that their writing is going public encourages students to revise in earnest. The booklets yield significant benefits for us, too. They help build a bank of student writing to draw upon in subsequent semesters. And as a bonus, the booklets allow us to reconnect with the experiences, thoughts, and feelings of the students passing through our classes year after year. Such booklets have been an ongoing source of pleasure.

A SUGGESTED SYLLABUS THAT INCLUDES THE MACMILLAN HANDBOOK

On the following pages we present a syllabus that will give you some further ideas on how to use THE MACMILLAN READER (MR). And for those of you who plan to supplement the MR with a handbook, we indicate ways that our book can be used with THE MACMILLAN HANDBOOK (MH). Note that the syllabus assumes the course meets once a week, for three hours, over a fifteen-week period. The syllabus can, of course, be easily adjusted to fit a variety of course formats.

Class 1

- Provide an introduction to the course and handle necessary business matters.

- Direct a getting to know each other activity (see page 2 of this manual).

- Have students prepare an in-class writing sample (see page 3) of this manual) to get an initial sense of their writing needs.

- Assignments--ask students to:

  a. Read "The Reading Process" in the MR.

  b. Read "The Writing Process" in the MR up to page 33.

Class 2

- Discuss assignments, including the activities.

- Return the in-class papers. Review common sentence skills problems and explain the way the MH can be used as a resource for developing such skills.

- Read and work through the rest of the writing process chapter.

- Introduce students to "Description," covering selected material on pages 59-71.

- Assignments--ask students to:

  a. Read the introduction to "Description" in the MR (pages 59-71).

  b. Read two of the five description selections, indicating which two. We suggest that the first selection should be "Wanting an Orange."

  c. Answer the close reading and craft questions which follow the selections and prepare to discuss the "For Further Thought" questions.

  d. Read "Writing the Whole Paper" in the MH as well as Chapter 31, Figurative Language."

Class 3

. Answer questions about the description chapter and discuss the two assigned description selections.

. Have students do prewriting (brainstorming, freewriting, group work, etc.) for one of the writing assignments at the end of the assigned description selections.

. Assignments--ask students to:

a. Complete the description essay.

b. Refer to the MH as needed for brushup work on grammar, punctuation, and usage.

c. Read Chapters 21 and 22 ("Sentence Fragments" and "Fused and Stringy Sentences") in the MH.

Class 4

. Initiate group feedback on students' description essays; see pages 4-6 of this manual. Give students the option of handing in their papers in present form or revising them by the next class.

. Introduce students to "Narration," covering selected material on pages 113-25 of the MR.

. Read and discuss in class a narrative selection: "Salvation" or "Handled with Care."

. Assignments--ask students to:

a. Read the introduction to "Narration" (pages 113-25) in the MR.

b. Read two more narrative selections, indicating which two.

c. Answer the close reading and craft questions which follow the selections and prepare to discuss the "For Further Thought" questions.

d. Read Chapters 26 and 27 ("Awkward Sentences" and "Wordy Sentences") in the MH.

Class 5

. Pass back and discuss students' description essays.

. Answer questions about the narration chapter and discuss the two assigned narrative selections.

. Have students do prewriting (brainstorming, freewriting, group work, etc.) for one of the writing assignments at the end of the two assigned narrative selections.

. Assignments--ask students to:

a. Complete the narrative essay.

b. Refer to the MH as needed for brushup work on grammar, punctuation, and usage matters.

c. Read Chapters 11-13 ("The Comma," "Semicolon and Colon," and "The Apostrophe and Other Punctuation Marks") in the MH.

Class 6

. Initiate group feedback on students' narrative essays;
   see pages 4-6 of this manual. Give students the option of
   handing in their papers in present form or revising them
   by the next class.

. Introduce students to "Exemplification," covering selected
   material on pages 171-86 of the MR.

. Read and discuss in class the exemplification selection
   "Allene Talmey."

. Assignments--ask students to:

   a. Read the introduction to "Exemplification" (pages 171-86)
       in the MR.

   b. Read two more exemplification selections, indicating
       which two.

   c. Answer the close reading and craft questions which
       follow the selections and prepare to discuss the "For
       Further Thought" questions.

   d. Read Chapters 15-17 ("Mechanics," Spelling," and
       "Agreement" in the MH.

Class 7

. Pass back and discuss students' narrative essays. Answer
   questions about the exemplification chapter and discuss the
   two assigned exemplification essays.

. Have students do prewriting (brainstorming, freewriting,
   group work, etc.) for one of the writing assignments at the
   end of the two assigned exemplification selections.

. Assignments--ask students to:

   a. Complete the exemplification essay.

   b. Refer to the MH as needed for brushup work on grammar,
       punctuation, and usage.

   c. Read Chapter 9 ("Parallelism, Balance, Antithesis")
       in the MH.

Class 8

. Initiate group feedback on students' exemplification
   essays; see pages 4-6 of this manual. Give students the
   option of handing in their papers in present form or revising
   them by the next class.

. Introduce students to "Process Analysis," covering selected
   material on pages 231-46 of the MR.

. Read and discuss in class a process selection: "How To Live
   to Be 200" or "The Beekeeper."

. Assignments--ask students to:

    a. Read the introduction to "Process Analysis" (pages 231-46) in the MR.

    b. Read two more process analysis selections, indicating which two.

    c. Answer the close reading and craft questions which follow the selections and prepare to discuss the "For Further Thought" questions.

    d. Read Chapter 28 ("Audience and Usage") in the MH.

Class 9

. Pass back students' exemplification essays. Answer questions about the process analysis chapter and discuss the two assigned process analysis selections.

. Provide prewriting (brainstorming, freewriting, group work, etc.) for one of the writing assignments at the end of the two process analysis selections.

. Assignments--ask students to:

    a. Complete the process analysis essay.

    b. Refer to the MH as needed for brushup work on grammar, punctuation, and usage.

    c. Read Chapter 19 ("Sentence Variety") in the MH.

Class 10

. Initiate group feedback on students' process analysis essays; see pages 4-6 of this manual. Give students the option of handing in their papers in present form or revising them by the next class.

. Introduce students to "Comparison-Contrast" or "Cause-Effect," covering selected material on pages 291-305 or pages 359-74. If appropriate, introduce the cause-effect activity described on page 74 of this manual.

. Read and discuss in class a comparison-contrast or cause-effect selection: "Male and Female" or "The Health Care System."

. Assignments--ask students to:

    a. Read the introduction to "Comparison-Contrast" (pages 291-305) or "Cause-Effect" (pages 359-74) in the MR.

    b. Read two more comparison-contrast or cause-effect selections, indicating which two.

    c. Answer the close reading and craft questions which follow the selections and prepare to discuss the "For Further Thought" question.

    d. Write a comparison-contrast or cause-effect essay.

    e. Refer to the MH as needed for brushup work on grammar, punctuation, and usage.

. Pass back and discuss students' process analysis essays.

. Answer questions about the comparison-contrast or cause-effect chapter and discuss the two assigned selections.

. Initiate group feedback on students' comparison-contrast or cause-effect essays; see pages 4-6 of this manual. Give students the option of handing in their papers in present form or revising them by the next class.

. Introduce students to "Definition" or "Division-Classification," covering selected material on pages 423-36 or 473-90.

. Read and discuss in class a definition or division-classification selection: "Entropy" or "In Depth, but Shallowly."

. Assignments--ask students to:

   a. Read the introduction to "Definition" (pages 423-36) or "Division-Classification" (pages 473-90) in the MR.

   b. Read two more definition or division-classification selections, indicating which two.

   c. Answer the close reading and craft questions which follow the selections and prepare to discuss the "For Further Thought" questions.

   d. Write a definition or division-classification essay.

   e. Refer to the MH as needed for brushup work on grammar, punctuation, and usage.

Class 12

. Pass back and discuss students' comparison-contrast or cause-effect essays.

. Answer questions on the definition or division-classification chapter and discuss the two assigned selections.

. Initiate group feedback on students' definition or division-classification essays; see pages 4-6 of this manual. Give students the option of handing in their papers in present form or revising them by the next class.

. Introduce students to "Argumentation-Persuasion," covering selected material on pages 547-75 of the MR.

. Read and discuss in class an argumentation-persuasion selection: "The Man in the Water" or "A Red Light for Scofflaws."

. Assignments--ask students to:

   a. Read the introduction to "Argumentation-Persuasion" (pages 547-75) in the MR.

   b. Read three more argumentation-persuasion selections, indicating which three. At least one of these selections (for example, "My Pistol Packing Kids" or "A Little Banning Is a Dangerous Thing") should focus on a controversial social issue; see pages 102-03 of this manual.

c. Answer the close reading and craft questions which follow the selections and prepare to discuss the "For Further Thought" questions.

d. Read Part Seven ("Sound Reasoning") in the MH.

Class 13

. Pass back and discuss students' definition or division-classification essays.

. Answer questions about the argumentation-persuasion chapter and discuss the three assigned argumentation-persuasion selections.

. Discuss the three argumentation-persuasion essays.

. Initiate prewriting (brainstorming, freewriting, group work, etc.) for one of the writing assignments at the end of the three assigned argumentation-persuasion selections. The writing assignment should require the student to focus on a controversial social issue; see pages 4-6 of this manual.

. Assignments--ask students to:

a. Complete the argumentation-persuasion essay.

b. Refer to the MH as needed for brushup work on grammar, punctuation, and usage.

c. If appropriate, read over Part Eight ("The Documented Paper") in the MH.

Class 14

. Answer questions about the argumentation-persuasion chapter and discuss the three assigned argumentation-persuasion selections.

. Provide group feedback on students' argumentation-persuasion essays; see pages 4-6 of this manual. Give students the option of handing in their papers in present form or revising them by the next class.

. Ask students to revise several essays written earlier in the course. These essays should be submitted in the final class; see page 7 of this manual.

. If appropriate, have students organize a forum on controversial issues; see page 102 of this manual for our comments on the activity.

. Assignment--ask students to prepare their oral presentation for delivery during next class' forum on controversial social issues.

Class 15

. Have students submit their folder of revised work.

. Have students deliver their oral presentations on controversial social issues.

. Provide group feedback on the the forum.

. Conclude the course.

Activities: Prewrite (page 22)

1.   Set A

    3 Abortion
    2 Controversial social issues
    5 Cutting off state abortion funds
    4 Federal funding for abortions
    1 Social issues

     Set B

    4 Business majors
    3 Students divided by major
    1 College students
    2 Kinds of college students
    5 Why many students major in business

Activities: State the Thesis (pages 26-28)

1. Limited subject: The ethics of treating severely handicapped infants

    FS Some babies born with severe handicaps have been allowed to die.
    TB There are many serious issues involved in the treatment of handicapped newborns.
    OK The government should pass legislation requiring medical treatment for handicapped newborns.
    A This essay will analyze the controversy surrounding the treatment of severely handicapped babies who would die without medical care.

  Limited Subject: Privacy and computerized records

    TB Computers raise some significant and crucial questions for all of us.
    FS Computerized records keep track of consumer spending habits.
    OK Computerized records have turned our private lives into public property.
    A In this paper, the relationship between computerized records and the right to privacy will be discussed.

2. Below are possible thesis statements for each set of points.

   Set A

   Possible Thesis: Students in college today are showing signs
   of increasing conservatism.

   * One evidence of this growing conservatism
     is the increased popularity of fraternities
     and sororities.

   * Beauty contests, ROTC training, and
     corporate recruiting--once rejected by
     students on many campuses--are again popular.

   * Most important, many students no longer
     choose careers that enable them to
     contribute to society but select, instead,
     fields with money-making potential.

   Set B

   Possible Thesis: If not monitored closely, experiments in
   genetic engineering could yield disastrous
   results.

   * We do not know, first of all, how
     engineering new forms of life might affect
     the earth's delicate ecological balance.

   * Another danger of genetic research is its
     potential for unleashing new forms of
     disease on the population.

   * Even beneficial attempts to eliminate genetic
     defects could contribute to the dangerous
     idea that only perfect individuals are
     entitled to live.

3. Below are possible thesis statements for each set of general
and limited subjects.

General Subject	Limited Subject	Possible Thesis
Music	Fads in Music	Musical fads rarely result in masterpieces that survive the test of time.
Psychology	The power struggles in a classroom	The classroom is often a battlefield, with struggles for power going on among students and between students and teacher
Politics	The separation of church and and state	Several frightening political groups advocate legislation that would compromise the separation of church and state.
Health	Doctors' attitudes toward patients	In hospitals, doctors often treat patients like robots rather than human beings.

1. Below are possible points of support for each thesis statement.

<u>Thesis:</u> The trend toward disposable, throw-away products has gone too far.

1. Fast food chains generate huge amounts of non-biodegradable refuse.
2. Parks and recreational areas are strewn with non-recyclable beer cans.
3. Roadways are littered with non-returnable soda bottles.

<u>Thesis:</u> All first-year college students should be required to participate in an orientation program conducted the week before the start of the academic year.

1. Such a program would familiarize students with the location of important campus buildings.
2. It would tell them about procedures for registration and advisement.
3. It would introduce them to other students, college officials, and instructors.

2. In each set below, the irrelevant point is preceded by an "X."

<u>Set A</u>

<u>Thesis:</u> Colleges should put less emphasis on sports.

    Encourages grade fixing
X   Creates a strong following among former graduates
    Distracts from real goals of education
    Causes extensive and expensive injuries

<u>Set B</u>

<u>Thesis:</u> America is becoming a homogenized country.

    Regional accents vanishing
    Chain stores blanket country
X   Americans proud of their ethnic identities
    Metropolitan areas almost indistinguishable from one
    another

1. Thesis: Our schools, now in crisis, could be improved in several ways.

I. Teachers
   A. Certification requirements for teachers
   B. Merit pay for outstanding teachers
II. Schedules
   A. Longer school days
   B. Longer school year
III. Curriculum
   A. Better textbooks for classroom use
   B. More challenging content in courses

2.   Thesis: Supermarket fruits and vegetables are far from
             being natural products.

     I. Techniques for growing produce
        A. Pesticide sprays in the fields
        B. Use of chemical fertilizers
     II. Preservative treatments in the warehouse or market
        A. Injections to retard spoilage
        B. Chemical dips to extend shelf life
     III. Cosmetic treatments in warehouse or market
        A. Dyes used to brighten colors
        B. Wax coatings to create shininess

DESCRIPTION

OPENING COMMENTS

Some colleagues tell us they prefer to omit description when they teach freshman writing. Emphasizing the analytic side of exposition, they consider descriptive writing a digression, a luxury that they don't have time for in an already crowded syllabus. To them, descriptive writing belongs in a creative writing course, not in freshman composition. On the other hand, some instructors do include description, but they discuss it after narration.

Both of us feel that descriptive writing should be included in freshman composition. And we've found that description can be covered before narration with excellent results. In other words, we recommend that description be the first pattern studied in the course.

Why do we feel this way? For one thing, when students begin by writing descriptive essays, they learn the importance of specific details, and they start to develop the habit of observation. (The sensory chart described on page 64 is one way to encourage such attention to detail.) Also, since descriptive writing depends on creating a dominant impression, description helps students understand the concept of focus early in the semester.

Descriptive writing also teaches students to select details that enhance an essay's central point. Finally--and most important--students can discover real pleasure in writing descriptive pieces. They are challenged by the possibility that they can make readers feel as they do about a subject. They enjoy using words to share with others a place, person, or object that has personal significance to them. Every semester, we have several students who admit that descriptive writing changed their attitude toward composition. For the first time, they see that writing, though difficult, can be rewarding and fun.

The selections in this chapter represent the wide range of techniques found in descriptive writing. We suggest you start with Woiwode's essay because its lushness dramatizes the way that vivid sensory details support a dominant impression. Likewise, the highly accessible essays by Trillin and Anderson show students how to select and organize descriptive details. These two pieces also illustrate the blending of subjective and objective description. Finally, we think that students will find Baker's "In My Day" and White's justly celebrated "Once More to the Lake" poignant renderings of personal experience. To create their effects, Baker and White use flashbacks, a technique usually associated with narration.

WANTING AN ORANGE

Larry Woiwode

1. Woiwode's thesis is implied. You might state it as: "The author's childhood memories of oranges reveal the fruit as special, beautiful, and a delight, not only to the taste but to the other senses as well."

2. The brothers loved oranges because in the cold, gray North Dakota winters, oranges were unusual. A tropical fruit, the oranges came from afar to remind them of the warmth and color of another climate. There are also implications that oranges were somewhat hard to get; they arrived in large shipments at the train depot, then appeared at the grocer's (10), and were brought to the house in bulk packed in crates or large net bags (4). Since the children had to make a special request for oranges, they were apparently not part of the daily fare. And, of course, the children loved oranges because they tasted good and were fun to peel and eat.

3. The boys enjoyed the orange almost as if it were a toy. They discovered that the spray from the fruit could be lit with a match "to create actual fireworks" (12); this game was heightened by the stealth required to play with forbidden items such as matches. Also, peeling the orange was something of a game-- "you might want to practice to see how large a piece you can remove intact" (13). An especially proficient orange peeler, such as the boys' father, might be able to remove the peel "in one continuous ribbon, so that ...the peel, rewound, will stand in its original shape, although empty" (13). And, of course, the oranges could be enjoyed before eating by appreciating their color, beautiful and bright in contrast to the purple tissue that wrapped them (11), their acid smell (10), and the feel of an orange in the hand (12).

4. Each method of orange eating has its own delights, Woiwode implies; also, no matter which way you eat an orange, "juice can always fly or slip from a corner of your mouth" (15). Woiwode describes three different ways of eating oranges. In the first, you have a choice of how you remove the peel. You can bite off the green nib and pick at the peel with your fingers, or pull the peel off carefully in one large ribbon. Once you have the orange peeled, you can divide the sections and then eat them (13-14). A second method is to slice the orange and eat the sections by digging your teeth into them to pull the fruit from the peel. A final method is to eat the orange whole. This method involves puncturing the peel, sucking out the juice, and then digging into the pulp and eating it until only the peel is left (16).

5. **degradation** (10): reduction to a lower status; demotion; debasement
   wended (10): proceeded, travelled
   elixir (10): a liquid solution that acts as a medical cure-all
   ingenious (13): inventive, creative, clever
   detonator (13): a device used to set off explosives
   morsels (14): small bits/pieces of food
   disembowel (16): to remove the insides of something

1. While Woiwode makes it obvious that oranges stimulate all
    the senses (except hearing), he spends almost three
    paragraphs on the sensuality of touching, peeling, and eating
    an orange, that is, feeling your lips "begin to burn from
    the bitter oil (13), the peel "abrade the corners of your
    mouth" (15), and the rind make "your numbing lips and the tip
    of your tongue start to tingle and swell up..." (16). Sight
    runs a close second to touch, with visual details found in
    paragraphs 11, 12, 14, and at the end of 16.   The author may
    have focused on touch to emphasize that eating an orange was
    an "event," an experience that surpassed the obvious tasting
    of the fruit.

2. Woiwode sets up a brief narrative frame for his
    description--the scene of his brother's and his scheming to
    get an orange. Within the body of the description, the
    overall organization is chronological, with a switch to a
    kind of emphatic order at the essay's climax. Starting in
    paragraph 10, the oranges come closer and closer. beginning
    with the arrival of the fruits at the depot, their appearance
    at the grocer's, on the dining table and in the Christmas
    stockings (11). Finally, at the start of paragraph 12, the
    author holds an orange in his hand, and then he describes the
    several methods of eating one. This climax of the essay is
    organized in a reverse emphatic order, with Woiwode's
    favorite method coming first, and the least significant
    coming last (13-16).

3. Imaginative comparisons abound in the essay. Some
    examples are: the comparison of the smell of oranges in the
    depot with "a renewing elixir" that rinsed the building (10);
    each orange vivid "as a pebbled sun" (11); "a whole pyramid
    of them in a bowl" (11); digging in your stocking "as if
    tunneling down" to China (11); the spray as a "watery
    fireworks" (12); "a mist like smoke" (12); the fruit as "a
    globe" (13); the center stem "like a mushroom stalk" (14);
    miniature sections "like babies being hatched" (14); "the
    slivers of watery meat" (15); "you can disembowel the orange
    as if it were a creature" (16); "oranges, soiled o's, light
    from afar" (16). Overall, the metaphors expand the
    significance of the humble orange to the grandeur of the sun,
    a pyramid, fireworks, and a globe to suggest how the oranges
    expanded the dark world of the author's childhood winters.

4. The conversation in the introduction and conclusion
    provides a frame for the essay. It draws us in because we
    are likely to be curious that children would feign illness to
    get an orange; we may be intrigued by the implied contrast
    with our own world, where jets make oranges commonplace year
    'round. The conversation also helps readers to accept the
    three-page depiction of an orange in all its glory, and
    focuses on the theme of how the scarcity of oranges in the
    American Midwest of the forties meant a great appreciation of
    their many sensuous qualities.

IN MY DAY

Russell Baker

<u>Questions</u> <u>for</u> <u>Close</u> <u>Reading</u> (p. 84)

1. The dominant impression is implied. You might state it
    as: "Parents rarely share the important memories of their
    upbringing with their children; only when it's too late do
    the children realize how little they know their parents."

2. Mrs. Baker believed in telling people exactly what was on
    her mind (11) and in taking on life's tasks with
    determination and energy (14). In her old age, she raged at
    the boredom, weakness and loneliness of being elderly (40)
    until she became senile. Then she began to dwell in the past
    with the ferocity and energy typical of her personality.

3. Baker felt "forever out of touch" with his mother in her
    last years because he realized that he knew so little about
    her life, the life she was sketching for him in her random
    flights into the past. He writes, "Of my mother's childhood
    and her people, of their time and place, I knew very little.
    A world had lived and died, and though it was part of my
    blood and bone I knew little more about it than I knew of the
    world of the pharaohs" (49). He also felt out of touch with
    his children, because he recognized that he had shared his
    own past with them only to "stun" them with how hard his own
    childhood was (50).

4. Living in the past was Mrs. Baker's only comfort in her
    infirmity. When Baker realized this, he stopped trying to
    get her to return to the unpleasant reality of her loneliness
    and kindly allowed her to live freely in the past. He even
    tried to follow along with her to learn about her life (44).

5. <u>inconceivable</u> (4): unlikely, unbelievable
    <u>libertine</u> (15): a morally unrestrained person
    <u>banal</u> (41): unoriginal, trite
    <u>wrest</u> (44): take or extract by force
    <u>exemplary</u> (50): serving as an illustration
    <u>galled</u> (51): irritated <u>consign</u> (58): to hand over

<u>Questions</u> <u>About</u> <u>the</u> <u>Writer's</u> <u>Craft</u> (p. 85)

1. Baker describes three memories of his mother in senility,
    interspersing between them images of her as a young, vital
    mother and of her as a bored, weak old woman. This
    alternating between images of her previous vitality and her
    weakmindedness helps us to understand what her son has lost
    as she has deteriorated mentally, and also helps create the
    dominant impression that understanding our parents'
    experiences is an important part of understanding ourselves
    that should not be left until it is too late. Specifically,
    Baker begins by giving us a brief description of an encounter
    he had with his mother after her bad fall, in which she
    thinks he is a stranger because he is so old (1-9). Then he
    provides some flashbacks to her as a young mother, so that we
    can understand the woman he expects her to be (10-15). The
    second example of her inability to focus on the present is
    the doctor's interview in paragraphs 17-39. This scene is
    followed by a description of her in an intermediate stage,
    before her "last bad fall," when she was aged, infirm,
    lonely, and unhappy (40-43). Baker concludes with a third
    scene of her meandering through the past, during which Baker
    felt it was most charitable to let her remain in the past; he
    even tried to follow her into bygone days.

2. The quotations of Mrs. Baker's own words are probably the most memorable aspects of Baker's portrayal of what she was like as a young mother and as a mentally frail old woman. These direct quotations allow us to know her youthful personality: "I tell them what I think whether they like it or not" and "If they don't like it, that's too bad." We learn in a direct way that while she is senile, she is still spunky: "You may know a lot about medicine, but you obviously don't know any history."

3. Repeating the words "she ran" is Baker's way of conveying to us how energetically his mother went about getting her life in order. She was, he says, "determined to bend those who opposed her..." (14), and her running everywhere was a sign of her frantic attempt to control her children, her household, and her life. This overabundance of energy, however, typically got her into trouble: she often tripped and fell; these falls serve to remind us of our ultimate mortality. The first incident occurred when she was a young woman running upstairs with a Thanksgiving turkey; her fall left her badly burned. Other falls occurred, we know, because she became bedridden after what Baker calls her "last bad fall." The repeated references to the falls contribute a sense of poignancy and coherence to the selection.

4. Mrs. Baker's comment is ironic because it is she who, in the end, wanders back mentally into the past. Her children, like most children, reject the past in order to move forward into their futures. As Baker points out, in his youth he "instinctively
...wanted to break free, cease being a creature defined by her time, consign her future to the past, and create [his] own" (58). Other ironies include her belief that Baker is too old to be her son (5); her knowing her own birthday and a rhyme about Guy Fawkes Day when she also fails the doctor's "reality" quiz "catastrophically" (33-38); her "knowing how to stare at a dolt" even though she herself is senile (39); and her recapturing her happy youth in senility.

THE BUBBLE GUM STORE

Calvin Trillin

Questions for Close Reading (p. 93)

1. The thesis is best represented by Trillin's comments in paragraph 2: "Still, the atmosphere in the store seemed unique. The people who ran it, a couple named Ken and Eve, were young, but the store was old-fashioned." While some students may feel the first sentence of the essay conveys the dominant impression ("...I became aware that a corner grocery store in our neighborhood was being operated with peculiar warmth"), Trillin indicates in the second sentence ("I don't mean...") that he does not consider it a viable statement of his main idea.

2. Trillin humorously notes one similarity to other corner
    groceries: "the place seemed to have the predictable
    inventory...cat food" (2) And, like many other small stores
    in his neighborhood, the owners are friendly. In many other
    ways, however, the store is unusual. The owners have not
    modernized it--the floor is worn linoleum and the cash
    register stands on a marble counter near the rear of the
    store. There are many personal touches--a wooden rocker,
    four different gum ball machines, freezer doors covered with
    decals and polaroids, plates of cookies on the counter, and a
    bookcase of used books free for trading. What Trillin calls
    the "air space" is filled with handmade ceramic mobiles and a
    clown who cycles across the store on a tightrope. More
    significantly, besides these decorative distinctions, the
    Bubble Gum Store is a meeting place: the owners make a
    practice of introducing customers to one another, for
    example. Finally, Ken and Eve make decisions about their
    store on the basis of what is good for the store's atmosphere
    as well as for its profitability.

3. "Neighborhoodism" refers to the sense of community that
    city dwellers in "lowrise" areas often nurture on their
    blocks. Unlike in the past, when neighborhoods were held
    together by ethnic homogeneity, the "neighborhoods" Trillin
    refers to are defined purely by geographic locale and are
    created by the mutual interest and commitment of the
    residents. Seeking a "casual neighborliness," a "qualified
    urban version of what people in other parts of America would
    consider a normal life," such residents start block
    associations, plant trees, hold block parties, and so on (4).

4. Ken and Eve may someday improve the store and conquer the
    routine of managing it to the point where being shopkeepers
    is no longer much challenge. When this happens, "they may
    sell out and move on" (12). This possibility suggests that
    Ken and Eve view the store primarily as a means of personal
    fulfillment rather than a way of making a living. For them,
    running the store is an act of creativity.

5. purveyor (1): distributor, supplier
    amass (3): accumulate, gather
    ethnic (4): pertaining to a religious, racial, or
                national group
    exclusionary (4): characterized by exclusion or
                      rejection of people or ideas
    overtly (5): obviously, visibly
    impromptu (7): spur-of-the-moment, unexpected
    patronage (8): clientele, customers
    assemblage (9): an artistic arrangement of
                    miscellaneous objects
    periodically (11): regularly

Questions About the Writer's Craft (p. 94)

1. Readers cannot skim or rush through Trillin's essay--the
    sentences force you to slow down and take your time, as
    Trillin reveals detail after detail about the store and sorts
    through the shopkeepers' motivations for running it. The
    style is slow-paced and relaxed, much as we imagine the store
    itself to be. Trillin's tone, while leisurely, is also
    objective and analytical. Thus, the long sentences and
    lengthy paragraphs both contribute to our understanding of
    what it feels like to visit the Bubble Gum Store and allow
    Trillin a vehicle to delve into the nature of the store, its
    owners, and the phenomenon of "neighborhoodism."

2. Through this comparison and contrast introduction, we are led to feel as intrigued as the author by a shop that stands out in a neighborhood of unusual stores. By describing other neighborhood stores first, Trillin establishes what is the usual thing in his neighborhood--friendly stores carrying speciality items. Then, he can show that even in this rather personal, small-shop neighborhood, the Bubble Gum Store stands out as unique.

3. Up through paragraph 3, Trillin discusses the neighborhood store's uniqueness and admits to a growing curiosity about its owners. In paragraph 4, he launches into a lengthy analysis of Ken and Eve's motives in starting the store, even discussing Ken's past and personality in some depth. The transition to this phase of the essay is marked by a space between the paragraphs and the transitional phrase, "As it turned out...."

4. Trillin provides a brief narrative of Ken's life (5) and how Ken came to buy the store (6); interspersed with the author's discussion of Ken and Eve's philosophy of shopkeeping are some other anecdotes: for example, how Ken came to buy the first gum ball machine "to warm the place up a little" and how even adults ask for change of a nickel to use the machines (8). These short narratives reinforce the idea of the store's specialness, which derives, clearly, from the special point of view held by its owners: their commitment to human warmth and personal excellence.

ONCE MORE TO THE LAKE

E.B. White

Questions for Close Reading (p. 102)

1. White's thesis is implied. One way of stating it is as follows: "In taking his son to revisit the lake where he experienced so many significant childhood events, White learns that he can only partly recapture the feelings and the atmosphere of days long past. Instead, he gets in touch with a premonition of his own death."

2. White suggests that his return to the lake was rather casual and impulsive (1). While he normally preferred the ocean, he says, sometimes the turbulence of the sea made him long for the calm of a placid lake in the woods. In addition, he could take his son along and introduce him to fresh water fishing. On a deeper level, he seems to have longed to revisit a place of significance from his youth and to share its pleasures with a son.

3. In paragraph 4, the author lies in his bed, hearing his son sneak out in the dawn light to take a motorboat out on the lake, just as White had himself done as a boy. His son's behavior is so similar to his own as a youth that he suddenly feels as if "he was I, and therefore...that I was my own father." Another significant transposition occurs when they are fishing (5). A dragonfly, an unchanging element of nature, alights on his rod and gives him the dizzying feeling

that he has moved back in time, until he "didn't know which rod [he] was at the end of." Finally, in paragraph ten, he identifies deeply with his son's attempts to gain mastery over the motorboat; he feels again all the same feelings he had in his youth as he grew to have a "spiritual" relationship with the motor.

4. The visit shows that things have remained much the same through the years. Nature has not changed much, nor has the town or the accommodations. In fact, White feels that the visit reveals the "pattern of life indelible" (8). Some details have changed, however, in keeping with the times. For example, the road has only two tracks, from the tires of automobiles, not three, from horse-drawn carriages (7); also, the boat is a modern outboard, not the one- and two-cylinder inboard motors of his youth. The waitresses are still country girls, but they have been impressed by the actresses in the movies and keep their hair cleaner than the waitresses of the past (7). Finally, the store serves Coke rather than old-fashioned sodas like Moxie and sasparilla (11).

5. incessant (1): continuous, not stopping
   placidity (1): peacefulness, calmness
   primeval (3): primitive
   transposition (4): a reversal or switching of place
   undulating (6): rippling, moving in wave-like fashion
   indelible (8): permanent, unerasable
   petulant (10): irritable, grouchy
   languidly (13): lifelessly, spiritlessly, without energy

Questions About the Writer's Craft (p. 103)

1. White presents the descriptions of the present day lake very objectively. "There was a choice of pie for dessert, and one was blueberry and one was apple, and the waitresses were the same country girls...the waitresses were still fifteen; their hair had been washed, that was the only difference--they had been to the movies and seen the pretty girls with clean hair." But White's descriptions of the past are sensuous and evocative, full of imagery that suggests they are more powerful than the present images. The memories of the past overtake and dominate the present experiences.

2. In paragraph 2, White calls the lake a "holy spot" and recalls a memory of the lake at dawn, when the woods along the shore seemed to form a "cathedral." Later, in paragraph 10, he describes the experience of learning to operate a motorboat as getting "really close to it spiritually." His description of the summer at the lake in paragraph 8 uses prayer-like language: "pattern of life indelible," "summer without end." These images convey White's almost religious reverence for nature: its beauty, peace, and permanence.

3. This passage uses the metaphor of a melodrama for the storm. This comparison points out that the storm is full of noise and turbulence but, in reality, is not dangerous. The storm's "audience," the children, in particular, get all excited about it, but to White, an old hand at the lake, the storm's "drama of electrical disturbance" is familiar. The storm is a joyfully scary event; the "gods grinning" suggests a pagan image of nature gods playing with the elements just for fun. The campers celebrate by running about and swimming in the rain. There is a serious undercurrent to the storm, however. While a harmless imitation of danger, it nevertheless sets the stage for White's premonition of death in the next paragraph.

4. The feeling grows out of a complex of events. The
   mock-danger of the storm has intensified everyone's
   reactions. White has enjoyed the storm as a piece of
   theatre; he remains on the sidelines wittily analyzing the
   scene. But the storm arouses the vitality of his son, who
   joins the frolicking campers. This action is the final
   example of how the son is growing up and away from his
   parent. (The boy takes the boat out by himself, for example.)
   When White feels a "sympathetic" iciness in his groin as his
   son dons his cold wet swimsuit, he is on one level
   identifying sensuously (again) with the boy's experience. In
   "biblical" terms, a child is the fruit of its father's
   "groin," and so the iciness also represents White's sudden
   awareness that his vitality is decreasing; to use the image
   of the melodrama, his scene is ending, while his son is
   center-stage. The many transpositions of identity between
   father and son have hinted at this final thought; White
   feels more and more like his own father, who, we can assume,
   has died.

CHILDREN'S HOSPITAL

Peggy Anderson

Questions for Close Reading (p. 109)

1. The thesis or dominant impression of "Children's
   Hospital" is implied. One way of stating it might be: "The
   design of Children's Hospital is meant to create an
   atmosphere of cheerfulness and normality for the sick
   children and their families."

2. Light enters the hospital through a glass roof atop a
   nine-story-high central atrium. Also, each patient's room
   has a window covering half a wall that looks out on either
   the atrium or the city. The lobby features numerous potted
   trees, benches, a working fountain, and a quarry tile floor,
   creating a parklike effect indoors. Finally, the hospital
   contains a McDonald's restaurant, with its tables and chairs
   arranged in an outdoor cafe within the lobby.

3. The major halls are arranged along the atrium, which is
   visible through glass partitions. As a result of this
   design, the halls are filled with natural light and permit a
   view across the court to patients' rooms, playrooms, waiting
   rooms, and offices. The overall effect contradicts that of
   most hospital hallways; these are not hushed passageways
   through the private realms of patient rooms and clinics, but
   open, light, public areas. The halls are filled with sounds
   that filter up from all levels of the hospital, and benches
   running along the glass walls encourage visitors and patients
   to congregate outside the rooms.

4. The designers used color extensively in the six floors of
   the hospital that are devoted to patients' rooms and
   treatment clinics, but didn't decorate the upper three
   research floors. In some patient rooms, orange circles
   enliven the ceilings, and bright stencilled letters mark
   bins; red and blue paths of linoleum run gaily through the

halls (12). Waiting areas contain child-sized furniture in
orange and green. Such use of color, Anderson says, "is
meant to lift heavy spirits" in the children's wards. Its
absence on the upper three floors creates a white, sterile
world, one appropriate to laboratories devoted to
experimentation and research.

5. edifice (1): building
    atrium (1): an open central court of a building
    siblings (4): brothers and sisters
    province (5): territory
    aggregate (9): conglomeration
    abounds (12): is plentiful in amount
    unobtrusively (12): quietly, inconspicuously
    odoriferous (13): giving off an odor

Questions About the Writer's Craft (p. 109)

1. Anderson provides many details supporting the impression
    of openness and light. Her description of the central court,
    lobby, hallways, and windows shows that the hospital is
    filled with sunlight and possesses an unusual sense of space
    (1-3, 6, 7-8). Details about color occur in paragraph 12.
    Other details in the article indirectly supplement this
    dominant impression: they pertain to the layout of the
    hospital (4-6, 13), the dispersion of sounds (8-9), and the
    hallway "cultures" (10-11).

2. Numerous transitions of space assist the reader to stay
    oriented. Some examples are: "Across the floor from
    McDonald's..." "At some remove from the pit and
    right next to the main entrance..." (4); "Beneath
    the cafeteria..." "The floor below that..." "Short
    wings off the lobby..." (5); "Each wall opposite
    ..."(6). Anderson also repeats key words to keep us aware
    of where w are when she discusses details. The word "lobby"
    provides continuity in paragraphs 1 - 3; "halls" appears
    frequently in 6 - 7 and 10; and "benches" provides coherence
    in paragraphs 10 - 11.

3. The sounds that contribute a sense of life and normality
    are described in paragraphs 8 and 9: a baby crying, a child
    requesting french fries and a milk shake, the fountain
    splashing, and many other noises. Anderson does not discuss
    smells, however, until she moves to the top floors, where
    there are "odoriferous laboratories" (12).

4. Anderson is concerned mainly with the hospital's impact
    upon its clientele--the patients and their families. This is
    clear from her relegating the description of the research
    floors to one paragraph. The contrast between the two parts
    of the hospital is dramatic and piques reader interest; in
    this sense, the conclusion is memorable. Finally, the
    description of the research floors' atmosphere as "quiet and
    white, as after heavy snow" creates an effective resting
    point.

NARRATION

OPENING COMMENTS

In our classes, we introduce narrative writing <u>after</u> description because we have found that descriptive writing helps students acquire many of the skills needed to write engaging narratives. For example, through descriptive writing, students discover the need to generate evocative details, use varied sentence structure, and establish a clear point of view.

Also, we often encounter students who are reluctant to write a narrative at the very start of the course. Schooled in the belief that a lightning bolt will strike them if they use "I" in an essay, they are more comfortable starting with description because it lends itself more easily to the objective third person point of view. (Obviously, both narration and description can be written in either the first or third person, but beginning writers tend to associate narration with the first and description with the third person.)

Even if it is not the first pattern covered, we suggest that narration be introduced near the beginning of the course. Everyone, after all, likes a good story, and most students have written narratives in high school and so feel comfortable tackling them in college.

Despite some students' familiarity and seeming ease with the narrative pattern, it's a good idea to keep in mind that narration requires a sophisticated repertoire of skills. Pacing, the choice of details, the telescoping of time, point of view: all offer a real challenge.

Students seem to have particular trouble understanding point of view. Because they tend to be more familiar with the first rather than the third person, we've found it useful to ask them to write two versions of the same narrative--one in the first and one in the third person. Such an assignment shows students how point of view changes a story and makes them aware of the advantages and limitations of each perspective.

Although each narrative in this chapter is filled with drama and tension, students find special power in the conflicts underlying Orwell's "Shooting an Elephant" and Hughes' "Salvation." Greene's piece, in addition to its welcome balm of optimism, helps students understand effective pacing. Watkins' essay, especially his story of animals' death throes, dramatizes the importance of vivid sensory impressions. And Sizer's detailed account of one day in the life of a high school English teacher illustrates how to condense time for maximum narrative effect.

SHOOTING AN ELEPHANT

George Orwell

Questions For Close Reading (p. 133)

1. Orwell's thesis is implied. One possible way of stating
    it is: "Imperialistic rulers must behave so as not to lose
    face or power over the populace, even if it means doing
    something against their better judgment."

2. Orwell felt pressured by the people, almost overwhelmed
    by their power over him through their mere presence. In
    theory, he explains at the start of the selection, he "was
    all for the Burmese and all against their oppressors, the
    British" (2). But, in reality, he felt the common people of
    the country were "evil-spirited little beasts who tried to
    make my job impossible" (2). During the shooting incident
    the people were "happy and excited," he says, and they
    watched him "as they would a conjurer about to perform a
    trick." He resentfully saw himself as having to spend his
    life "trying to impress the 'natives'" (7). He reports
    later that, as he fired a shot, the crowd emitted a "devilish
    roar of glee" (11). His choice of words shows that he
    resented and disliked the Burmese.

3. Orwell shoots the elephant because the two thousand
    native people standing behind him expect him to. They want
    vengeance for the man it killed, the meat the carcass will
    provide, and the entertainment of watching the shooting. "The
    people expected it of me and I had got to do it" (7), he
    writes. There is an implication that if he decided not to
    shoot the elephant, both he and the empire would suffer a
    loss of prestige, but the main concern in Orwell's mind is
    the "long struggle not to be laughed at" (7). He is even
    afraid to "test" the animal's mood by going closer for fear
    it might attack and kill him before he could shoot, thus
    giving the crowd a sight it would enjoy as much as the
    slaughter of the beast.

4. Despotic governments result from the need to maintain
    power over subtly resistant people; such a government can
    rule only by fulfilling the people's expectations and
    responding to every crisis with the expected force. Orwell
    points to the irony that he stood armed in front of an
    unarmed crowd, yet he was powerless to do as he wished or as
    his judgment told him. Instead, he felt himself "an absurd
    puppet pushed to and fro by the will of those yellow faces
    behind" (7).

5. imperialism (2): a country's policy of gaining power
                          by acquiring and ruling territories
    prostrate (2): lying face down, as in submission or
                          adoration
    despotic (3): tyrannical, all-powerful
    mahout (3): the keeper and driver of an elephant
    miry (5): swampy, muddy
    conjurer (7): magician
    futility (7): uselessness, ineffectiveness
    sahib (7): "Master"; Indian title of respect when
                          addressing Europeans

Questions About the Writer's Craft (p. 134)

1. What Orwell calls a "tiny incident" lasted only a short
   time, perhaps only an hour at most. Orwell uses clear
   transitions of time to keep us oriented as to what is
   happening, but he provides no specific clock time. "Early
   one morning," the narrative begins (3); after the death of
   the coolie, the action steps up and the transitions indicate
   things are happening at a rapid pace: "...he could not have
   been dead many minutes..." (4); "As soon as I saw the dead
   man..." (4); "the orderly came back in a few minutes..." (5);
   "meanwhile some Burmans had arrived..." (5); ""As soon as I
   saw..." (6); "I thought then..." (6); ""But at that
   moment..." (7); "And suddenly I realized..." (7); "And it was
   at this moment..." (7); "I perceived in this moment..." (7);
   "But I had got to act quickly..." (8); "For at that moment"
   (9); "When I pulled the trigger..." (11); "In that instant,
   in too short a time..." (11); "He looked suddenly
   stricken..." (11); "At last, after what seemed a long
   time--it might have been five seconds..." (11); "And then
   down he came..." (11). In paragraphs 12 and 13, Orwell
   describes the refusal of the animal to die: "I waited a long
   time..." "Finally I fired..." "...but still he did not die"
   (12). The incident ends with Orwell leaving the scene but
   learning later that the animal took half an hour to die.

2. The first two paragraphs introduce us to the alien,
   far-off world where the narrative took place. In addition to
   setting the scene, Orwell explains what he was doing in Burma
   and, more importantly, gives us an emotional perspective from
   which to view the event. We learn in a general way about the
   bitterness between the colonialists and the native
   inhabitants and about the psychological effect his job as a
   policeman had on him. His confession that he was "young and
   ill-educated" and not even aware the British Empire was
   collapsing helps us feel empathy for him in the incident that
   follows. Without this information, we might not be willing
   to forgive him the shooting of the elephant or its horrible
   death, or comprehend the sense of victimization he felt
   despite his position as an "authority."

3. Orwell uses analogies in three important places. Two of
   the analogies are from the theater and relate to the sense
   of falseness that Orwell feels about his role in the colony.
   With the crowd watching him, he compares himself to "a
   conjurer about to perform a trick" with "the magic rifle."
   Then he helps us to understand his own psychological state at
   that moment by using another theater image: "Here was
   I...seemingly the lead actor of the piece; but in reality I
   was only an absurd puppet pushed to and fro by the will of
   those yellow faces..."; in the East, he says, the white man
   "becomes a sort of hollow, posing dummy....He wears a mask,
   and his face grows to fit it" (7). Paragraph ten continues
   this analogy, as Orwell describes the crowd breathing "a
   deep, low, happy sigh, as of people who see the theatre
   curtain go up at last." The third analogy compares the
   elephant to an elderly person; as he watches the beast in the
   rice paddy, he feels it has a "preoccupied grandmotherly
   air." After he fires the first shot, he says the elephant
   "looked suddenly stricken, shrunken, immensely old.... His
   mouth slobbered. An enormous senility seemed to have settled
   upon him. One could have imagined him thousands of years
   old" (11).

4. Orwell vividly evokes the suffering of the elephant by carefully observing the animal's movements after the shot. He notices the subtle but "terrible change" that came over it, in which "every line of his body had altered." The analogy with an old man helps structure his observations that the elephant seemed paralyzed, then sagged to his knees and slobbered. Other trenchant details include the image of the animal standing "weakly upright" again and the image of him toppling "like a huge rock," "his trunk reaching skywards like a tree," and trumpeting once (11). In paragraph 12, Orwell provides a graphic description of the beast's death agony. He reports firing over and over; into a picture that has so far been in black-and-white, he interjects colors. He remembers that the elephant's "mouth was wide open" so that he "could see far down into caverns of pink pale throat," and that "the thick blood welled out of him like red velvet." In this paragraph, too, we hear sounds: the "tortured breathing," the "dreadful noise," and the "tortured gasps" that continued "steadily as the ticking of a clock."

HANDLED WITH CARE

Bob Greene

Questions for Close Reading (p. 139)

1. Greene's thesis is implied. Some possible versions are: "A troubled person's deviant action can arouse the pity and concern of onlookers, who may realize that, deep down, they are not so very different." Or, "Our everyday normal world is really very fragile, for any one of us could easily cross over the line into deep disturbance. Or, "So-called 'abnormal' behavior, such as walking naked on a city street, is really a cry for help. People do well to treat such behavior with compassion and sympathy."

2. The newspaper describes a scene of voyeurism and titillation; it obviously desires to play up the sensationalism of a nude woman strolling on Michigan Avenue. Greene's investigation of the event indicates, however, that the atmosphere was calm and almost solemn. From his point of view, the real story is not the woman's disrobing, but the gentle, concerned reaction of the passersby and their intuition that the woman is deeply troubled.

3. The passersby watch her sadly; other than that, they do not react. "No one jeered at her or attempted to touch her," Greene writes (11). No one tries to help her until the police arrive. They catch up with the woman on the Michigan Avenue Bridge and cover her up immediately; rather than arrest her, they take her to a mental health clinic.

4. Greene recognizes that violating a social rule or norm is a sign that a person desperately needs help (8). The woman chooses a peaceful, non-destructive signal of her desperation.

5. titillation (7): arousal, stimulation, excitement
   trifling (9): insignificant, minor
   blissful (10): extremely happy or joyful

<u>Questions</u> <u>About</u> <u>the</u> <u>Writer's</u> <u>Craft</u> (p. 140)

1. Greene creates narrative tension by describing the events
    of the woman's walk slowly, almost step-by-step. He doesn't
    tell us how the stroll came to an end until the last few
    paragraphs. Instead, he fills in the details of the scene; he
    introduces onlookers, even giving the name and occupation of
    one of them, and includes their various observations about
    the woman. He also interrupts his narrative to quote John
    Barth and to relate the woman's behavior to the fine line
    between sanity and disturbance in all of us. You could say
    his description of this event is as leisurely and
    unsensationalistic as the stroll itself. This pace keeps us
    eager to learn how the walk ended. The conflict that
    underlies the narrative is that between an individual's
    self-expression and our society's rules, in particular, the
    rules that govern how we present ourselves on the public
    streets. Another conflict occurs between the two media
    reports, the first the sensationalistic newspaper account
    and the second, Greene's more reflective column.

2. The onlookers and the police handle the woman with care,
    that is, with understanding. Greene also handles her with
    care in writing about her gently and compassionately. We are
    conditioned to expect that the woman would be treated
    brutally by society, but the title emphasizes that the
    unusual thing that happened on Michigan Avenue was that
    people responded sympathetically and not cruelly to a
    troubled person.

3. Barth's words help us understand how thin the line is
    between normality and emotional collapse and enable us to
    relate to the woman's inner motives. Through this quotation
    we can appreciate that feeling close to breakdown is a
    universal experience. Greene includes the excerpt along with
    the bystanders' comments to help articulate their sense that
    the woman was disturbed. Like the onlookers, we can share in
    the feelings of fragility and sadness as we follow the rest
    of her walk.

4. Greene seems to have interviewed the observers himself;
    he uses direct quotations from them (6). He may also have
    examined the police reports, but he does not say.
    Nevertheless, the precision with which he describes the naked
    woman's route and her every action gives him great
    credibility; most students will find his report more
    authoritative than the newspaper account. Besides describing
    the events, Greene also probes the woman's possible motives
    and the meaning of her action for all of us. He is, in other
    words, interested in the feeling level of the events, not
    just the reporter's facts.

LITTLE DEATHS

T.H. Watkins

Questions for Close Reading (p. 148)

1. Watkins' thesis is implied. One way of stating it is:
    "'Trapping varmint' to help ranchers and farmers is a cruel
    way of making a living that blunts a person to the meaning of
    death and suffering."

2. Watkins, a "practicing student of western history," was
    fascinated by the tales of adventure told about mountain men,
    whom he considered "hopelessly romantic creatures" (3). His
    cousin, while not actually a descendant of such men, and not
    in any way similar to the grizzled stereotype of a trapper,
    was still a kind of mountain man. Watkins says he was
    "entranced with the notion" of accompanying him on his rounds
    (3).

3. The cousin has numerous positive qualities: he pursues
    his job in a businesslike and efficient manner; he is
    obviously not a "mean killer." His answers to Watkins'
    questions show him trying to be cooperative and honest about
    the details of his work. When a dog is found in a trap, the
    cousin rightfully shows anger at the irresponsible people who
    turn dogs loose. He makes an attempt, after Watkins suggests
    it, to free the dog, and then when he cannot, he kills it in
    the most painless way (20-26). Finally, Watkins shows us
    that the cousin likes children and goes out of his way to
    bring them the pleasure of petting a new-born lamb (31).
        The cousin chose trapping because hunting and gunning ran
    in his family; his choice of a job was consistent with the way
    he had been raised. His father, whom the cousin "worshipped
    and emulated," according to the author, had been a state
    trapper and had risen to trapping supervisor. The family
    "had been killing things for a long time," Watkins says (6).
    In addition, the cousin has an aversion to civilization, so
    much so that he considers the isolated hill country of his
    current assignment too crowded for his taste (30).

4. The incident of the dog differs from the others because,
    first of all, the dog is still alive and Watkins must witness
    the animal's death by pistol, and also because dogs are not
    the intended prey of the traps. The trapping of the dog is a
    mistake, and this animal's death cannot be rationalized, as
    can the deaths of "varmints" like skunks, raccoons, and
    foxes. Watkins describes the incident at length because it
    calls into question the rightness of trapping in general and
    displays the cruelty, unfairness and ugliness of this form of
    "pest control."

5. chaparral (2): a dense thicket of shrubs and small trees
    anarchic (3): uncontrollable, uncontrolled, wild
    predilection (3): tendency to like; attraction to something
    lineal (3): biologically related to or descended from
    emulated (6): strove to imitate and to equal
    encompassed (6): included, surrounded

Questions About the Writer's Craft (p. 148)

1. The deaths of the animals in paragraphs 8 and 14 are
    especially vivid. Watkins uses some irony in his choice of
    words to describe the first animal they find, the raccoon.
    He says it has a "small mouth, crawling with ants, open in a
    bare-tooth grin" and that "the tiny flies sang about
    the ragged wound" (8). This last image also appears in his

description of the dog's death: "The dog howled once, a long penetrating <u>song</u> of despair..." (26). In describing the death of the bobcat, Watkins points out the "torn circle of earth" left by the animal's rage. The most frightening detail is the "yellow tufts of...fur scattered on the ground, as if the bobcat had torn at its own body for betraying it" (14).

2. To help us keep track of events, Watkins uses time transitions as well as references to the time of day; often these appear with references to the trappers' location as well. Watkins begins with a description of the dawn in paragraph 5; the cousins' arrival at the first trap is indicated by a description of its location in space: "We got out of the truck and beat our way through the brush..." (8). Watkins begins paragraph 14 with a time transition, combined with references to the time of day and their spatial location: "By the time we reached the top of the long ridge...the morning had slipped toward noon...." At the start of paragraphs 15 and 16, he makes a transition to the second set of traps through a reference to their spatial movement. Sixteen also uses a reference to the time of day: "in the oven-heat of a strong spring sun..." and a transition of time: "By the time we were ready to approach the last three traps of the line, it was well after three o'clock. We were very high up by then...." The next transitions focus on spatial location (18, 19, 23). Finally, as the day draws to a close, Watkins uses a reference to the last trap to keep us oriented (27), and in paragraph 31, he lets us know that "there was plenty of light left when we got back...."

3. In paragraph 5, Watkins provides an overview of the mountain country as he and his cousin drive out to look at the traps; he says the "isolated bunches of cows and sheep stood almost motionless, like ornaments..." and that "the exposed earth of the road cut like a red scar...." Later in the article, he describes the noose-pole for subduing trapped animals as being "as thick as a broomhandle" and as looking "like a primitive fishing pole."

4. The cousin reveals a neutrality towards the "varmints" he traps--he shows neither sympathy nor malice toward them. His description of how the animals die is very complete, but also matter-of-fact: "Hunger, thirst, and shock is what kills them, mostly.... That, and exhaustion, I reckon" (8). We are able to detect touches of feeling in his use of profanity and slang; he shows some restrained self-satisfaction at the success of catching the pregnant fox and the long-sought-after bobcat: "Great....There won't be any little foxes running around this year" (13); "I"ll be damned....I"ve been after that bugger all month. Just about give up hope" (14). His annoyance and perhaps embarrassment at finding a large dog in one of the high traps comes through in his curse: "<u>Dammit</u>." In addition to revealing his cousin's unusual attitude toward the death of animals, the dialogue creates suspense in the climactic scene of the trapped dog. As a whole, these conversations reveal a world where the death of small animals is routine, a part of a job, not something to be mourned or fretted about; the conversations also contribute to supporting the thesis, for they show a world different from that of most of us, a world where "death is the only commonplace" (1).

SALVATION

Langston Hughes

<u>Questions for Close Reading</u> (p. 152)

1. The thesis in this selection is implied. You could state
    it this way: "As a boy, Langston Hughes pretended to be saved
    and lost his faith at the same time." Another way of
    expressing it is: "Religious fervor sometimes leads to
    religious hypocrisy and disillusionment."

2. There are many pressures on the young Hughes. He is the
    last child left on the "mourner's bench," the only one left
    unsaved, and he suffers shame (11) and guilt. His aunt, the
    minister, and the whole congregation pray for him "in a
    mighty wail" (7) and beg him to be saved. He feels the
    pressure of time passing (11) and that of the heat as well
    (6). Finally, Wesley invites him to join in a deception and
    gives him an example of a person who pretends to be saved
    without suffering any vengeance from God; Langston comes to
    understand that perhaps the only way to be saved is to
    pretend.

3. Wesley does not seem to be a believer, for he chooses
    deception without any qualms. On the other hand, Langston
    believes what his aunt has told him about salvation: you see
    a light, and Jesus comes into your life. Langston is patient
    and trusting, while Wesley is cocky and profane.

4. Auntie Reed sees only what she wants to see; hearing him
    crying in his bed the night of the revival, she believes he
    is emotionally overwhelmed by his religious conversion. She
    fully accepts the values of her church and takes the external
    event of walking from the mourners' bench to the altar as
    proof of salvation. She does not seem to have any
    understanding of psychology at all. If her nephew told her
    the truth of his experience in the church, one of two things
    would probably happen: he would convince her that he is a
    sinner because he had lied in church, or he wouldcause her
    to lose her faith as he has lost his.

5. <u>revival</u> (1): a meeting for the purpose of reawakening
                          religious faith
    <u>knickerbockered</u> (11): dressed in knickerbockers, full
                                pants gathered below the knee
    <u>punctuated</u> (14): emphasized, accentuated
    <u>ecstatic</u> (14): rapturously joyful and excited

<u>Questions About the Writer's Craft</u> (p. 153)

1. Hughes creates suspense by drawing out the description of
    his turmoil as the lone unsaved sinner for almost one-third
    of the essay (6-11). By this point, we already know the
    expectations his aunt and the preacher have for him, and he
    begins the portrayal of his shame by introducing the
    possibility of deception: Wesley's false salvation (6). We
    wonder throughout the next five paragraphs whether Langston
    will hold his ground, be saved, or lie. Another technique
    that increases the suspense is the use of very specific
    details about how he was pressured. He tells us the
    imagery of the songs sung the night of the children's meeting
    (3, 4). Also, he uses dialogue to show Wesley's irreverent
    invitation and to present the scene of the minister
    passionately calling him to the altar.

2.   Because he has the role model of Wesley's sacrilege, the
     narrator understands that lying is a safe option for him to
     choose. Wesley, in a sense, is his "salvation" from the
     shame of not being saved. Wesley also serves as a foil to
     Langston; by contrast, Langston's honest and trusting nature
     is all the more apparent. Learning that Wesley is proud
     about his deception, we can feel more strongly the poignancy
     of Langston's bitter tears.

3.   "The whole room broke into a sea of shouting,"
     Hughes writes, and "waves of rejoicing" filled the
     church. Through this metaphor, he portrays the unified and
     overwhelming force of the congregation as it engulfs the last
     converted sinner. The image also suggests Langston is
     helpless and even drowning in the religious ecstasy around
     him.

4.   The hymns sung at the children's revival meeting take on
     a personal meaning for the young Langston. We are told, for
     example, that one song is about a hundred lambs, of which
     ninety-nine are saved and one is left out in the cold (2). A
     second hymn provides an image of hell ("the lower lights are
     burning") to motivate "poor sinners" to be saved. The songs
     thus threaten the boy with the torments of cold and fire
     unless he comes to Jesus.

HORACE'S COMPROMISE

Theodore Sizer

Questions for Close Reading (p. 165)

1.   The thesis of this selection is implied. The narrative
     of Horace's day makes clear that his job keeps him intensely
     busy, leaving him minimal time to complete other important
     teaching-related tasks, such as preparation and feedback to
     students. One way of stating the thesis is, "A day in the
     life of a high-school English teacher shows that he does his
     job well because, first of all, he possesses great mastery of
     his subject, teenage psychology, and school politics, and
     secondly, he is willing to compromise some of his goals."

2.   Horace has settled into the familiar routine of an "old
     pro." Since he has seniority, he has a carrel to himself
     (younger or newer teachers must share); like other older
     teachers, he comes to school early, and he feels entitled to
     one free cup of coffee from the communal pot as a reward for
     his diligence. He goes about the business of switching from
     one class level and subject to another without much ado. He
     knows how to handle the rowdiness and sniggering of students
     (10, 13), and his attitude to the administration is assertive
     and self-assured (32). Most significantly, he steers his
     course confidently past the many obstacles in his
     way--disrespectful students, rigid administration,
     unavailable materials, and overwork.

3.   Clearly, most of Horace's day is spent in the classroom
     with students, but each day also includes a variety of other
     activities. He has one free period in his daily schedule,

the morning, at lunch, and during his free period he takes
every opportunity to join his fellow teachers in idle
chatter. Finally, working on student plays as adviser to the
set crew gives him great satisfaction.

5. semantic (7): pertaining to the meaning of words
   inordinately (9): excessively
   melodramatic (10): extravagantly emotional, overly dramatized
   kibitzers (25): givers of unwanted advice
   indecorous (26): improper, tasteless, indecent
   etymological (28): having to do with the history of words
   circumlocutions (29): roundabout ways of speaking
   felicitous (47): suitable to the occasion
   verbiage (47): quantity of words

Questions About the Writer's Craft (p. 166)

1. In providing direct dialogue, Sizer emphasizes grating
   and frustrating conversations between Horace and students or
   coworkers. Most of these direct conversations occur between
   Horace and his students. For example, in paragraph 8, we
   learn how Horace treats two latecomers to his class.
   Paragraph 9 shows Horace fielding some queries from reluctant
   students, and in paragraphs 11-15, Sizer provides some
   highlights of Horace's first class on Romeo and Juliet.
   Later, in paragraphs 19-21, we catch bits and pieces of his
   freshman grammar lesson. All of these dialogues show Horace
   coping with dull, recalcitrant, or giddy students. Sizer
   does not include any dialogue from the more mature
   third-period class or the advanced placement class.
   Likewise, the exchanges between Horace and other staff are
   also negative in tone: he has an embarrassing conversation
   with Miss Viola (27) and must assert himself with the
   assistant principal and negotiate with the teacher in charge
   of the book storeroom (32). The direct dialogue in the essay
   thus serves to spotlight Horace thinking on his feet, solving
   communication problems, and wrestling with unruly classes.
        By eliminating quotation marks, Sizer can condense the
   scenes and zero in on the most important parts of the
   dialogue: those that show Horace's tried-and-true strategies
   for handling problem classes, students, and administrative
   issues. This run-together style of presenting conversations
   makes them very easy to read and keeps the essay moving at a
   fast pace, in keeping with the teacher's busy day.

2. While Horace's day is certainly typical in many ways, the
   description of his personal habits and quirks convey that
   this is the experience of a particular person with his own
   individual style. For example, we learn that he drinks lots
   of coffee and smokes, but that he prefers chatting and
   but on this particular day, he has two other periods freed up
   by an assembly and by United Nations Week. He grades some
   student papers during the free period (33) and takes some
   others home (37, 39). At various times during the day, he
   relaxes in the teachers' lounge (6, 24-26) and in the
   cafeteria (31), and also briefly checks in with a colleague
   in the bookroom, another teacher, and an administrator. He
   also remains in his room a half hour after classes so
   students who wish to speak to him can find him easily. Then
   he joins the tech crew to help them plan the lighting for the
   upcoming student play, Our Town. In all these
   activities, only the casual chatting with other teachers is
   unrelated to helping students.

4. Horace seems to enjoy his job quite thoroughly, since he
   has resigned the chairmanship to be able to devote himself
   full time to teaching (2). In particular, he has one
   favorite, highly motivated class that he especially enjoys.
   Also, collegiality seems to be a major reward for Horace; in

gossiping with colleagues to joining in the on-going card
game in the teachers' lounge. In addition, many of these
details evoke the tedium and frustration of a teacher's day
and thus assist Sizer to develop his thesis.

3. Sizer begins by telling Horace's story because it draws
us into the concrete world of today's American high school
and tells us what teaching is really like from the front of
the classroom. This is important, because most readers have
experienced school only as students and have no sense of the
teacher's point of view. By getting inside Horace's teaching
day, readers can experience for themselves the conflict
between his innate devotion to educating young people and the
shortcuts necessitated by overwork and restless students.
Sizer thus leads the reader to identify with Horace and
become, presumably, more sympathetic to the plight of
American teachers. Also, providing the substance of a
teacher's daily experience draws us into the subject; readers
bored by school as students would most likely find an
analytic essay or book on the subject of school reform dry
and uninteresting as well.

4. This concluding discussion gives us a more complete view
of the teacher's life; it balances the purely narrative view
of what Horace does in school on one particular day by
summarizing his goals and ideals (41-42) and providing an
overview of his week (41-48). This objective and even
somewhat statistical outline shows how difficult it is for
Horace to fit all his duties into the time available in a
single week, and it reinforces the impression we have gained
from the narrative: that Horace is dedicated, overworked, and
pragmatic. Sizer thus uses this discussion to support his
main idea and increase our appreciation of the hard life of a
teacher. He further heightens our awareness of "Horace's
compromise" by repeating "Horace is realistic" throughout the
concluding section.

EXEMPLIFICATION

OPENING COMMENTS

When we first started teaching, both of us were caught off guard by students' seeming inability to provide detailed, specific examples in their papers. But we soon uncovered one reason for the vagueness of their writing. Many of them arrived in college with the notion that good writing is abstract and full of high-faluting language. And warned by dutiful high school English teachers against padding their papers, they often came to regard specific details and "for instances" as fluff.

We've found an almost sure-fire way to help students appreciate how powerfully examples can affect a reader. We have them react (see page 173-74) to two versions of the same student writing, one enlivened with specifics, the other flat, lifeless, and sorely in need of supporting details. When we question students about their reactions ("Which version is more interesting?" "Which version gives you more of a sense of the writer?"), we can almost see their eyes light up. Once the importance of vigorous supporting details is appreciated, we spend some class time on prewriting activities to help students learn how to generate raw material for their essays.

That skill mastered, some of our eager-to-please students then go overboard and give us too much of a good thing. They heap their papers high with too many examples, forcing readers to wade through a mass of specifics that don't lead anywhere. When this happens, we emphasize that writers need to be selective and choose the most striking examples to support a point.

Varied in subject and mood, the professional selections in this chapter illustrate the power to be found in writing richly supported by details. Both Packard and Nilsen tackle complex social issues with the aid of numerous illustrations. In a gentle, reflective essay, Lindbergh sometimes uses a string of specifics (see, for example, the eighth paragraph in "Channelled Whelk") to suggest the clutter of everyday life. Rollins' lively piece about an unforgettable boss dramatizes the value of selectivity—of finding just the right specifics. And the clear organizational plan of Cowley's essay (see the second paragraph) makes the "View from 80" accessible to students, most of whom are not even in their twenties.

CHILDREN AT RISK

Vance Packard

Questions for Close Reading (p. 192)

1. The first sentence provides an indirect statement of the
   thesis. A more direct version of the main idea would be:
   "While we think of our society as a very child-oriented one,
   in actuality some elements of our complex and cold society
   are as dangerous to the welfare of children as some clearly
   anti-child practices of the past."

2. Children in past centuries were dressed the same as
   adults. and were permitted the same access to all areas of
   life (the Brueghel painting suggests this). They were often
   forced to do "grown-up" work--performing manual labor or
   child-care duties for younger children. In other words,
   children were not viewed as having special emotional and
   physical needs.

3. Until this century, the turmoil of industrialization and
   urbanization and the harshness of the Calvinistic religion
   caused people to be very unsympathetic to children (6). A
   kind of "tenderness taboo" prevented adults from strong
   affection for their young, since the unsanitary conditions of
   the time meant a very high infant mortality rate. In
   addition, the Calvinists taught that children should be
   punished as harborers of Original Sin. These notions about
   children were challenged by the philosophers of the
   Enlightenment (23-24). Rousseau stressed that children were
   natural, healthy creatures, and Locke taught parents to treat
   their children with love and respect.

4. In the U.S., education costs run twice as high as in
   Europe; teachers number more than three million, including
   67,000 guidance counselors; and over 28,000 doctrors serve as
   pediatricians and over 3000 as child psychiatrists.

5. ideologies (1): systematic bodies of concepts
   urbanization (8): development into cities
   laissez-faire (14): without governmental interference
   congenial (25): agreeable or sympathetic
   malaise (27): sickliness, unhealthiness
   demographic (32): pertaining to human populations

Questions About the Writer's Craft (p. 193)

1. Packard relies much more on general examples than on
   statistics to make his point. Statistics do occur when
   Packard wishes to convey that in some ways the US is more
   child-centered than Europe (26), and also in his discussion
   of the growth of cities (9). Some specific details include
   those about the use of wet nurses in eighteenth-century Paris
   (17), the apprenticeship of small children (12), and the
   punishment of children who wet the bed (21). Packard does
   supply an extended example in paragraphs 16-19, where he
   discusses the specific case of young people's being used in a
   degrading and cruel fashion in British coal mines. At the
   end of the essay, when Packard discusses contemporary
   attitudes to children, there are few examples. He refers
   generally to "pains and problems" that "threaten to create a
   permanent warping of a large segment of our coming
   generation" (32), but he offers no examples of what he means
   by either "problems" or "warping."

2. At the end of the essay, we may wonder exactly how today's children are being harmed (or "warped") and what are the special consequences of the social ills Parkard cites (divorce, working mothers, and a "cool, hard world"). These unanswered questions would lead us to read on in his book.

3. Packard's tone is clearly ironic--while the adults of the nineteenth century may have believed such child labor was "character-building," Packard reports this attitude to reveal its cruelty. Packard uses irony elsewhere as well. In paragraph 15, he writes that "reformation" of the working laws "reduced" child labor to ten hours a day, indicating that by his standards, this was hardly a reformation at all. In paragraph 21, he notes "it was the Christian duty of their parents..." to purge children of evil by whipping; this comment conveys that this behavior does not coordinate with his view of Christianity.

4. The short paragraphs are very easy to read; each one introduces a new piece of information without much fanfare, and the pace of the essay is stepped up. The effect is something like that of reading a list of information. Packard's goal is to overwhelm us with the cruelty to children that has been the norm in Western civilization, and this rapid-fire delivery of facts helps him achieve this goal.

ALLEEN TALMEY

Betty Rollin

Questions for Close Reading (p. 199)

1. Rollin's thesis is implied. It could be stated as follows: "The toughest part of Vogue was Allene Talmey, the features editor. By being ferociously demanding on her staff, she insured the highest quality work would appear in Vogue." Or: "The toughest part of a tough magazine was the features editor, Alleen Talmey. While driving her staff hard and refusing to spare their feelings, she earned their respect and love as well as their fear."

2. Allene Talmey was the senior editor of the feature department; she supervised two secretaries and three writers, including Betty Rollin. Her job involved approving article ideas and evaluating drafts of articles; her overall goal was to maintain the high level of writing in the magazine.

3. With her high standards, Talmey would accept nothing less than perfection from her writers. She hated convoluted sentences that did not make their messages clear; she despised cliches, abhorred spelling errors, and mocked less-than-classy article ideas. All these errors signalled "slop," or worse, "ignorance" (10).

4. Her tone of voice, word choice, and gestures made anyone she dealt with "feel like a worm" (2). For example, she made the word dear take on the meaning moron by her ironic pronunciation, and she used a contemptuous, deadly tone to command revisions. And, Rollin adds, she never raised her voice. Her intimidating gestures included

standing to deliver a scolding and touching flawed
manuscripts as if they were physically soiled. Other
workers coped with this perfectionism in various
ways. The two secretaries simply did not make mistakes,
something possible for clerical help but not likely for a
writer. Rollin's coworkers reacted to Talmey's
critiques by being "lah-de-dah" or by not revealing
that Talmey's reprimands caused them pain. Rollin,
however, responded by closing her office door and
bursting into tears.

5. cower (1): cringe, shrink back
    convoluted (2): twisted, overly complicated
    cordial (5): friendly, warm-hearted
    excruciating (10): extremely painful

Questions About the Writer's Craft (p. 199)

1. Rollin organizes the examples according to the relative
    magnitude of the "sins." Writing convoluted sentences was a
    serious transgression, as writers' sins go, but nothing like
    using a cliche. And far worse than the "slop" produced by a
    writer who failed to correct her spelling was any sign of
    ignorance. This worst sin of all is dramatized by the "quiz"
    on general knowledge that Talmey inflicts upon Rollin. We
    are likely to be surprised that this senior editor of a
    woman's fashion magazine knows baseball statistics--in terms
    of "perfection," in other words, she is as demanding of
    herself as she is of her staff.

2. To show Allene Talmey from the inside would be to reveal
    her thoughts, her values, her humanness, but Rollin's goal is
    not to show her as a rounded human being. Instead, by keeping
    strictly to an external view of Talmey, Rollin emphasizes the
    interaction of a demanding boss and her employees, something
    many people can relate to. She also creates the image of
    Talmey as someone who never let down her guard.

3. Many of the sentences in the first paragraph are very
    short. They indicate that the atmosphere at Vogue was
    one of urgency and drama, and they mirror the rapid, powerful
    effect Talmey had on her staff: "We crumbled. We shriveled.
    We dissolved." A second feature of this paragraph that you
    might want to discuss is the repetition of the word "tough"
    (five times). Besides this being an unusual word to apply to
    a high-class fashion magazine, the repetitions pound the
    notion of toughness into our minds.

4. Such terms as "beating," "meat grinder,' "sin," and
    "transgression" convey the intense effect Talmey's rebukes
    had on her staff. These images do seem humorously
    exaggerated, as do some of the comparisons Rollin uses to
    describe Talmey's contemptuous gestures: she touches a
    less-than-perfect manuscript "as if it had been used to wrap
    a flounder" (5) or "as if it were a soiled bedsheet" (2) and
    lets "each syllable drip like slime" (5) when she discusses a
    cliche in the author's writing. These comic comparisons
    suggest the affection that underlies the author's dread of
    her boss. As she said in the first paragraph, she loves
    Talmey.

THE CHANNELLED WHELK

Anne Morrow Lindbergh

Questions for Close Reading (p. 207)

1. Lindbergh's thesis is implied. One way to express it is as follows: "A life with a simple shape, like that of the shell, is best; it leads to a feeling of being 'in grace,' to being 'at peace with oneself' (5)." Or: "Women's lives would be improved if they could minimize the complications and distractions that go along with being wives, mothers and career women; they might then find inner harmony."

2. The shell, first of all, reminds her of the creatures it housed, a sea snail and a hermit crab. Then, she admires its simple beauty, its color, texture and shape. It is a simple, useful, and beautiful object.

3. Women perform several roles in life, as mothers, wives, and homemakers; in the modern world, they can also choose to be involved in community affairs and the professions (8). The problem of multiplicity does not affect men so much, because their lives have been more restricted to professional and community affairs; they have had far fewer responsibilities in the home. "Distraction is, always has been, and probably always will be, inherent in woman's life."

4. Although Lindbergh says she "could live in it always" (19), she must leave the beach house to return to her everyday responsibilities, her chosen life of wife and mother. She takes the shell of the channelled whelk with her to remind her of its message of simplicity. She also hopes it will encourage her to aspire to inner harmony and grace (21).

5. apex (2): pointed end, tip
   conducive (6): apt to produce or bring about
   myriad (12): a great number; various
   periphery (12): outskirts or surrounding area
   sedentary (17): marked by much sitting

Questions About the Writer's Craft (p. 208)

1. The major use of extended example occurs in paragraphs 14 to 17; here, Lindbergh moves away from discussion and analysis to provide the specifics of what she has shed at the beach. Earlier, in paragraph 7, she has included an extended example of "the caravan of complications" that characterize the life of a modern woman.

2. By beginning with an evocative description of the shell, Lindbergh conveys a powerful image of a natural, simple kind of life. These images provide an inviting introduction to the essay and also contrast with her description of her own busy, "blurred" and barnacled woman's life (3). In paragraph 13, she returns to the image of the shell, stating specifically that it gives her a clue about how to achieve balance. In paragraphs 19-21, she meditates upon it one last time, hoping the shell will continue to inspire her to seek "grace" in life once she takes it back to Connecticut with her.

3. "Tying a shoestring" stands for all the trivial but
   absolutely necessary duties people must perform to survive.
   At first, Lindbergh uses the phrase off-handedly--"one can
   hardly tie a shoestring"--to refer to how frustrating and
   difficult ordinary tasks can be when one is feeling "out of
   grace." By repeating the image in the next sentence, she
   lets us know she is using the phrase as a metaphor for life's
   drudgery.

4. In speaking directly to the shell, Lindbergh treats it as
   if it were a being or a presence in itself. In the previous
   paragraph, she discusses how the shell's message of
   simplification pertains to the "outside" of her life. In
   addressing the shell, she indicates it has become part of her
   inner life and has set her thoughts on an inward journey of
   awareness and change.

SEXISM AND LANGUAGE

Allene Pace Nilsen

Questions for Close Reading (p. 216)

1. Nilsen states her thesis very broadly at the end of
   paragraph two: "Anyone living in the United States who
   listens with a keen ear or reads with a perceptive eye can
   come up with startling new insights about the way American
   English reflects our values." Students may wish to refine
   this statement; here is one possibility: "American English
   is sexist, for it contains many words with negative
   connotations for females and just as many words with positive
   connotations for males."

2. In English, animal terms commonly applied to women
   usually imply negative qualities, such as undesirability,
   ugliness, aggressiveness, or meanness. On the other hand,
   similar animal-derived terms applied to men tend to be
   neutral or to emphasize positive qualities such as physical
   strength, intelligence, or competence. Nilsen supplies
   complementary instances of this phenomenon in paragraphs 3
   and 4. For example, a shrew is a nagging woman, but shrewd
   means an astute and clever person, as in a "shrewd
   businessman" (3).

3. Different job names serve to glorify men's work and
   minimize the significance of women's work, even when the
   tasks performed are the same. Serving food, for example, is
   a waitress' job in most restaurants, but in the armed forces,
   food is served by orderlies, who are really just male
   waitresses under a different name. Likewise, Nilsen points
   out, the armed services have men assigned to be
   clerk-typists, medics and adjutants, positions called
   "secretary," "nurse," and "assistant" in civilian life and
   normally performed by women. Outside the armed forces, men
   become chefs and tailors, while women performing the same
   duties are called cooks and seamstresses. The different sets
   of terms tell us that men do not want to be identified with
   any typically female activities, and they will do certain
   jobs only when they are retitled with a masculine-sounding,
   "higher-status" name (13).

4. Positive terms for women emphasize youth, beauty, and sweetness. Nilsen gives as examples terms derived from words for baby animals (8), food (20), and flowers (21). Such terms suggest women are either sexually seductive, passive and fragile, or nonhuman pets or objects. The many masculine associations with words for violence ssem to be a result of the reality of our culture--most violence is committed by men (17-18). As Nilsen says. "We have very negative feelings toward someone who is hurting us or threatening us or in some way making our lives miserble. To be able to do this, the person has to have power over us and this power usually belongs to males" (18).

5. unscrupulous (5): immoral, unprincipled
    enticing (7): alluring, attractive, seductive
    connotation (8): implied (suggested) meaning
    virile (11): masculine, manly; having the strength
                 and energy of a man
    lexical (15): relating to words
    maudlin (15): overly sentimental; weepy
    vigilante (16): a citizen without authority who pursues
                    and punishes criminals

Questions About the Writer's Craft (p. 217)

1. Each point Nilsen makes is bolstered by myriads of examples. Since we may never have noticed these patterns of positive and negative connotations in our language, we might be surprised and doubtful about the validity of her ideas. But Nilsen overwhelms any such objections by supplying so many specific instances of what she means. She clearly recognizes that our tendency to ignore the characteristics of our own language may make us resist the notion that language itself can be sexist. With so many examples at hand, Nilsen can take on the most suspicious anti-feminist and convince him (or her) that our language contains many negative judgments about women.

2. Nilsen examines the use of negative animal terms for women and positive ones for men (3-6, 8-10), the positive connotations of descriptive terms for male characteristics (11, 16), and the application of object-nouns to women (20-21). These three motifs are introduced to us in the headings that divide the essay. These headings serve as transitions; they also outline the organization and tell us the next main idea we are going to encounter.

3. Beginning with animal terms for humans allows Nilsen to start the essay dramatically. These animals terms are the most blatant, shocking, and--in the case of terms applied to women--degrading examples of sexism in language. We are likely to be intrigued and shocked by the contrasts between "shrew" and "shrewd," "lucky dog" and "bitch," and eager to read on. The section lets us know that the essay is not going to be a dry analysis of English semantics, but a presentation of ideas that affect us on a gut level.

4. Throughout the essay, Nilsen maintains a neutral, analytic tone. She establishes this tone of seriousness at the outset, by putting her ideas in the perspective of cultural anthropology, and she continues it by using

objective terminology, avoiding loaded words, and qualifying
her statements: "...not only a mixed metaphor, but also
probably the most insulting animal metaphor we have"
(4); "Other animal metaphors do not have definitely
derogatory connotations for the female, but they
do seem to indicate frivolity..." (6); "Probably
the most striking examples..." (9). Also, her use of
headings contributes to the sense that we are reading a
formal report on research. Nilsen avoids a stuffy or
impersonal tone, however. She often refers to her audience
through the use of the first-person plural: "Most of us
feel..." (4); "We see it in our animal metaphors ...(8); "The
names we give to young children..." (14). She also
occasionally speaks directly to her readers: "Look at the
differences between..." (6); "Now, how can the Marines ask
someone who has signed up for a man-sized job to do
women's work?" (13).

Despite this tone of objectivity, Nilsen is very open about
her own point of view on sexism in our language; she says,
for example, "...I was shocked to discover that we have
remnants of this same attitude in America" (8). In large
part, Nilsen conveys her point of view implicitly; in
paragraph 3, for example, she says quite neutrally that "we
can uncover some interesting insights into how our culture
views males and females," yet the examples she offers shock us
into understanding her view that English debases women.

THE VIEW FROM 80

Cowley

Questions for Close Reading (p. 225)

1. Cowley states his thesis in the first sentence of
   paragraph two: "In his new role the old person will find
   that he is tempted by new vices, that he receives new
   compensations (not so widely known), and that he may possibly
   achieve new virtues."

2. The "vices" of old age are avarice, untidiness, and
   vanity, according to Cowley. Older people are tempted by
   avarice because, he suggests, they are in a stage of life
   when all seems to decline; the only power they have that may
   remain unaffected is the power to hoard (3). Untidiness may
   result partly from lethargy, the author says, but also from
   an over-valuation of the remnants of long-past events (6).
   Vanity is the easiest vice to explain; older people yearn to
   be recognized for their successes in life, no matter how long
   ago they occurred (7). This need leads old people to display
   their ancient trophies, wear their school letters, dye their
   hair, and drop "innocent boasts" into the conversation (8).

3. The aged enjoy pleasures that baffle the young and
   active. Cowley says that one pleasure "is simply sitting
   still...with a delicious feeling of indolence that was seldom
   attained in earlier years" (10). Many simple activities
   become deep joys: eating (11), drinking, or remembering the
   past. Other old people enjoy engaging in silent imaginary
   conversations wtih vanished friends and relatives (12).

4.   Cowley tells us outright at the end of paragraph 15 that
      "the men and women I envy are those who accept old age as a
      series of challenges." He then provides examples of people
      who conquered the infirmities of age and continued their
      creative lives. Such people ignore pain and weakness and
      find ways to compensate for incapacities.

5.   menopause (1): the end of menstruation, occuring in mid-life
      obstinate (2): stubborn, closed-minded
      lethargy (6): tiredness, sluggishness
      nirvana (11): bliss; peaceful spiritual state
      infirmity (16): feebleness, sickliness
      atrophy (17): deterioration

Questions About the Writer's Craft (p. 225)

1.   Cowley uses a number of striking examples, any of which
      students might find memorable. Certainly, the story of
      Langley Collyer's trash-filled house will stick in many
      readers' minds, as will the examples of artists and writers
      who persevered in their crafts despite great physical
      difficulties: Renoir, Goya (16), and Papini (17). Cowley
      seems to use quotations for two purposes--first to show that
      his "view from eighty" is not unique, and then to demonstate
      the unusual vitality of some people in old age. The
      quotations from Gide (1) and Cicero (9) back up two of
      Cowley's points about the feelings of the elderly. The
      segment of an Emerson poem also reveals feelings of decline
      that some elderly people are likely to have, although Cowley
      points out that Emerson himself did not really share them
      (13). The surprising quotations at the end of the piece
      demonstrate the rare determination of certain aged painters
      and writers: Renoir claimed, "You don't need your hand to
      paint," and Goya portrayed an aged man with the inscription,
      "I am still learning" (16). Cowley concludes with a shocking
      statement by poet Paul Claudel, who insisted that a person
      can do "astonishingly well" without sight, hearing, teeth,
      mobility, or breath (18).

2.   Cowley quotes Gide's idea of old age as a "role" in order
      to give his readers a sense of how incongruous it can feel to
      be a youthful spirit in an aging body. The inner self
      remains the same; the person has put on the makeup of the
      elderly. The adjustments and "improvisations" involved in
      taking on this role lead to the new vices, pleasures, and
      virtues that Cowley discusses in the essay.

3.   The essay's organization is emphatic. Cowley moves from
      the less important point, vices, to a more significant aspect
      of being old, the pleasures, and then on to his main focus,
      the importance of continuing to achieve in old age. The
      thesis sentence provides a preview or map of this
      organization.

4.   Cowley's tone in the essay is friendly and basically
      light. He treats the foibles of the aged with humor and
      acceptance and takes pains to explain many aspects of old-age
      in detail. He writes as if his audience consists of younger
      people--people in middle age, perhaps--who may be ignorant,
      fearful, or prejudiced about old age, or who might be in need
      of some reassurance that old age is not so dreadful as they
      fear.

<u>PROCESS ANALYSIS</u>

OPENING COMMENTS

Like many of our colleagues, we cover process analysis
early in the semester. This pattern of development teaches
students a great deal about selectivity ("Which steps should I
cover?" "How many examples should I provide?"), organization,
and transitional signals. Process analysis also highlights the
importance of audience analysis. To explain the steps in a
process clearly, the writer must identify what readers need to
know and understand.
Students often expect process analysis to write itself;
they expect it to unfold naturally and automatically. But once
they get feedback on their first draft, they realize that the
sequence of steps was self-evident only to them and that they
need to work hard to make the process accessible to their readers.

This chapter includes process analyses that vary widely
in subject and time. We usually start with Leacock's essay,
finding that students enjoy the essay's humor and get a kick out
of learning that health fanatics are not a new breed. In
addition to providing a laugh, Leacock's "How to Live to be 200"
also illustrates the use of the imperative to explain a process.
Roberts' tongue-in-cheek essay prompts similar laughter and
also shows students that humor can be used to make a serious
point. Unlike the lighthearted response elicited by Leacock and
Roberts, "The American Way of Death" evokes shock and even
repulsion. Mitford's unforgettable piece underscores the
effectiveness of highly specific details. Finally, the essays by
Hubbell and McWilliams illustrate the way a step-by-step sequence
can be rearranged to achieve an intended effect.

HOW TO LIVE TO BE 200

Stephen Leacock

<u>Questions for Close Reading</u> (p. 250)

1. The thesis of the selection is implied; you might state
   it as: "If you want to live to 'enjoy a grand, green,
   exuberant, boastful old age (13),' you should ignore health
   fads like exercise and special diets and just relax."

2. The "Health Habit" is a collection of behaviors that
   supposedly promote longevity. To take "Jiggins" as an
   indication, the health habit includes "cold plunges," "hot
   sponges," and numerous exercises. Monitoring your diet is
   another aspect of this habit.

3. Leacock notices that people who eat right often avoid
    many common foods because of concern over possible ill
    effects (10). He mockingly calls them "cowards" because they
    are "afraid" of such items as oysters and alcohol.

4. Comfort, not health, should dominate your activities,
    Leacock implies. He recommends not getting up early, but
    waiting until the last possible moment, for example, and
    eating all you can afford to pay for. As far as exercise is
    concerned, he recommends watching as much athletics as you
    like.

5. ozone (10): pure, refreshing air
    pepsin (10): a digestive enzyme
    cholera (17): a fatal disease characterized by stomach disorders

Questions About the Writer's Craft (p. 250)

1. Opposing the usual health-fad instructions for dieting
    and exercising, Leacock provides a counter set of
    commandments for good health. His use of the imperative
    gives him the same air of authority as the health
    faddists--his tone is commanding and assertive. Since his
    recommendations are far-fetched, the effect is one of
    mockery.

2. Leacock conjures up the process of becoming fit according
    to the health fanatics, and he also explains, on the other
    hand, how to enjoy life. Both processes are intended to
    produce a long, healthy life, and the essay implicitly
    contrasts them.

3. Exaggeration creates much of the humor in the essay.
    Leacock's portrait of the typical behavior of the health
    maniac is exaggerated, for example; "He got so he could open
    and shut his pores at will..." (2); "He could have got a job
    as a dog anywhere" (4). Also, many of Leacock's
    recommendations are tinged with hyperbole: "Eat what you
    want. Eat lots of it. Yes, eat too much of it..." (19);
    "...it is only a fad of modern medicine to say that cholera
    and typhoid and diphtheria are caused by bacilli and germs;
    nonsense..." (17). Such broad statements add humor and show
    that Leacock thinks our concern with health is itself out of
    proportion.

4. The sentences in "How to Live to be 200" are mostly
    declarative or imperative and simple in structure. Even when
    complex, the sentences are fairly short and create a
    fast-paced rhythm. The sentence style also contributes to
    the comic effect because Leacock uses this blunt, almost
    dictatorical style to tell us to do what we are probably
    doing anyway--relaxing and enjoying our lives.

THE BEEKEEPER

Sue Hubbell

Questions for Close Reading (p. 255)

1. Hubbell's thesis is implied; one way of expressing it
   might be, "Beekeeping is an unusual, satisfying occupation."

2. Hubbell's previous helper has moved away, so she has
   recruited David, the son of friends. He is a strong young
   man accustomed to physical labor--important because
   harvesting honey is heavy work. From his behavior in
   accepting bee stings, we know he is brave and eager to please
   as well.

3. Desensitization is the process of becoming so used to bee
   venom that the skin no longer reacts with redness and
   itchiness. Since getting stung by angry bees is inevitable,
   honey harvesters must be desensitized to the stings. While a
   bee worker gets used to being stung and becomes unafraid of
   it, desensitization does not prevent a person from feeling
   the pain of the sting--as we learn when Hubbell tells us
   about her previous summer's helper contorting his face
   grotesquely when several bees stung his forehead.

4. The supers are wooden boxes located above the hives where
   the bees store excess honey that they will not need for the
   winter. These boxes, while heavy, can be moved away from
   the hive and are the source of the honey to be harvested.

5. enzymes (3): proteinlike substances formed in plant and
   animal cells which serve as catalysts for
   various processes
   bulbous (6): rounded or swollen
   pulsate (6): throb
   densensitize (6): make less sensitive
   anaphylactic (7): a condition of hypersensitivity caused
   by previous exposure

Questions About the Writer's Craft (p. 256)

1. The process of making and gathering honey is really two
   processes, the first performed by bees, the second by humans.
   Bees make honey in a four-step process: they collect nectar
   from flowers; enzymes in their bodies change the various
   sugars to the simple sugar of honey; young bees fan the honey
   once it is deposited in the hive to evaporate moisture and
   thicken it; then, the bees seal each cell of the honeycomb
   with wax. In the second process, Hubbell and her assistant
   gather the honey by removing the supers from above the hives,
   blowing off the bees, and taking the supers to the honey
   house. There, Hubbell has machines that slice open the
   honeycombs, spin the honey free, and pump it to containers.

2. Hubbell defines many terms of the trade so her readers
   can visualize the harvesting process: honey house, power
   uncapper, extractor (2); supers, bee blower (4);
   protective clothing (5); desensitizing (6-9);
   and bee stinger (6). She does not bother to define
   the possible serious effects of bes stings, such as
   such as anaphylactic shock, because to do that would take
   her too far from her subject.

3. She interrupts the narrative of David's introduction to the work of bee keepers to tell an anecdote about her previous assistant (12-14). This anecdote reveals the loyalty she and her worker felt towards each other, and it serves to dramatize the fellowship that lies ahead for her and David.

4. Although she never says it directly, Hubbell clearly finds beekeeping an interesting, special business. The first paragraph shows her pride in her work--not only the health inspector will be proud. Her enjoyment also comes across in her playful comments. For example, she likes to insinuate to people that she is really running a still in the woods (2) and she states that she is a good boss who will help her worker in distress rather than go and get a cup of coffee (14). Finally, the loving attention to the details of her machinery, the bees' behavior, and the process of desensitization show her belief that beekeeping is a significant business worth knowing about.

THE AMERICAN WAY OF DEATH

Jessica Mitford

Questions for Close Reading (p. 264)

1. Mitford's thesis is implied by her introductory comments that "Embalming is indeed a most extraordinary procedure..." (1) and that it is very difficult to obtain information about what goes on behind the "formaldehyde curtain" (3). One way of stating the thesis might be: "Americans should know exactly what they are paying for when they have a relative embalmed." Another version might be: "Knowing the details of embalming is every American consumer's right and responsibility."

2. Ignorance about embalming has a number of causes. On a pragmatic level, bookshops and libraries do not stock texts on the subject, Mitford says (1). Also, while at one time deceased people were prepared for burial at home with a relative standing by, our current custom is to hand over the body to "professionals" who perform their rituals in the mortuary. Mitford suspects that morticians would discourage any family member who wished to witness the procedures because they do not want the information about embalming to become widely known. In addition, the author points out, the law forbids others than the family or mortuary students to watch. Finally, while Mitford says she doubts "the secrecy surrounding embalming can... be attributed to the inherent gruesomeness of the subject" (2), since everything from heart surgery to birth is televised these days, students will probably admit to some squeamishness about the subject themselves.

3. Mr. J. Sheridan Mayer reminds us that the goal of mortuary science is to present the deceased in a lifelike manner: "Our customs require the presentation of our dead in the semblance of normality...unmarred by the ravages of illness, disease or mutilation" (11). Mitford's treatment of this notion is ironic. After quoting Mayer's guidelines, she makes the wry comment, "This is rather a large order since few people die in the full bloom of health...."

4. The dead person's body can be made to look even better
    than when he or she was alive by repairing visible damage
    caused by illness or acccident. In paragraph 12, Mitford
    grimly describes the remedies taken if a body part is missing
    or if the face is bruised and swollen: replacements are
    fashioned out of wax, heads are sewn back on with the
    stitches hidden under a high collar or scarf, and swollen
    tissue is cut out from the inside. Additionally,
    emaciation's ravaging can be repaired, Mitford explains in
    paragraph 13, through the injection of cream, and the effects
    of diseases on skin color can be rectified through cosmetics,
    colored lights and careful attention to color-coded casket
    interiors (15).

5. docility (1): the quality of being easily led or managed
    intractable (3): stubborn
    reticence (3): silence, unwillingness to speak
    augers (5): tools for making holes
    distend (5): to stretch, expand, or inflate something
    stippling (12): applying by repeated small touches
    jaundice (15): an illness characterized by a yellowish
                    discoloration of the body

Questions About the Writer's Craft (p. 264)

1. There are two main stages in the process of preparing the
    body for the funeral. First it is embalmed. This is the
    procedure by which blood is replaced with "about three to six
    gallons" of some sort of embalming fluid (9) and body fluids
    in the torso with "cavity fluid (10)." The deceased's eyes
    are closed with cement, the mouth sewn shut, and the face
    "creamed" to protect it from burns by the caustic embalming
    chemicals (10). The second stage of the process,
    restoration, occurs eight to ten hours later. During this
    stage the mortician, using the combined skills of a sculptor
    and a cosmetician, repairs the appearance of the body and
    makes it look lifelike. This process involves making casts
    of missing limbs (12); modeling the face to be neither too
    emaciated or too swollen (12-13); positioning the jaw,
    perhaps by dislocation, so the lips stay shut (14); and
    finally, washing, shaving (if male), shampooing, and dressing
    the body (16). The final step of this process is "casketing"
    (17).
        Mitford uses very clear transition words to delineate
    the steps of the two stages, embalming and restoration.
    Embalming is described sequentially, so she uses transitions
    of time and addition: "The body is first..." (4) "another
    textbook discusses..." (7); "a contrasting thought is offered
    by another writer" (7) "To return to Mr. Jones..." (8);
    "meanwhile" (9); "the next step is..." (10). Mitford also
    employs repetitions of sentence structure to signal she is
    adding detail to detail: "There are cosmetics, waxes and
    paints...There are ingenious aides..." she writes in
    paragraph 5. "If Flextone is used..." (8) and "If he should
    be buck-toothed..." (9) are other examples of this strategy.
    Mitford uses this transition technique again in the section
    on restoration, where details are added in response to a
    series of similarly worded questions and conditional clauses:
    "Is a hand missing?..." "If a lip or two, a nose or an ear
    should be missing..." "Head off?..." "Swollen mouth?..."
    "If too much is removed..." (12); "If Mr. Jones happens to
    have no teeth..." (14) "If Mr Jones has died of jaundice,
    does this deter the embalmer?..." (15).

Mitford separates the two stages of the mortician's job by devoting the end of paragrqaph 10 to making the transition: "He had beeen embalmed, but not yet restored." And, in paragraph 12, Mitford orients us to the start of the second stage by stating, "The embalmer, having allowed an appropriate interval..." (12). The discussion of restoration uses many transitions indicating contrast: "The opposite condition..." (14); "however" (14); "on the other hand" (15 and 17); and of addition: "another method" (14). Paragraph 14 begins with a reference to "a problem," so that we know the paragraph will discuss its solution process. Also in this section, there are some transitions referring to process: "sometimes..then... "(14). Many other details, however, are piled on without transition (16 and 17). Paragraph 16 begins with a summation of the process so far and moves us on to the next stage: "The patching and filling completed, Mr. Jones is now shaved, washed and dressed...." And paragraph 17 introduces the last stage by a transition of process: "Jones is now ready..." (17).

2. "Mr. Jones" is an "everyman" name; using it for the corpse conveys that this procedure is univerally applied in our country. The name also gives the dead man an identity--it is a constant reminder that this is a human being, being subjected to grotesque and dehumanizing techniques. We can feel shock and shame as these processes are performed on a "Mr. Jones" instead of on a "body." The use of the particular name helps Mitford draw her readers over to her point of view. However, Mr. Jones is never given any particular physical characteristics, life history, or cause of death, so that, while he is a person, not just a dead body, he could still be any person.

3. The quotations from mortuary science textbooks let us know that Mitford has done her homework; she has acquired some of those hard-to-get books on embalming and studied them. The quotations thus increase her authority on the subject. Since the process of embalming is a mystery to most of us, the quotations verify the almost incredible details of the procedures (see paragraphs 12, 15, 16, 17), and convey the theory behind the process as well (6, 7, 11). The particular quotations often combine the subject of barbaric mutilation with a self-congratulatory or sanctimonious tone. The style is usually excessively pompous and marked by terminology designed to underscore the logicality or necessity of the procedures: "It is necessary to..." "removes the principal cause of..." (6); "for every hour that elapses...will add to the problems..." "we must conclude that..." "In the average case..." "One of the effects of..." (7); "Our customs require...." "This is the time..." "all doubts of success vanish..." "It is surprising and gratifying..." (11).

4. For the most part, Mitford's tone is reportorial; she describes the odd and fantastic processes without much comment or overt interpretation. Occsionally, however, there are touches of irony and sarcasm, enough so that one can tell that Mitford is not objective about the funeral industry. For example, her discussion of how to place the body in a coffin is clearly meant wryly: "Proper placement of the body requires a delicate sense of balance. It should lie as high as possible in the casket, yet not so high that the lid, when lowered, will hit the nose." She points out that placing the body too low will cause the body to look as if it is in a box. Likewise, the questions in paragraph 12 mock the mortician's blase attitude toward dead bodies: "Head off? ...Swollen mouth?" Also, her word choice can be evaluative, as in paragraph 5: "_appropriately_

corrupted...as 'demisurgeon'" "equipment...crudely
imitative of the surgeon's..." "a bewildering array of
fluids...." Finally, her choice of quotations from texts in
the field certainly contributes to our sense that
practitioners of mortuary science are self-aggrandizing and
pretentious, if not actually charlatans.

HOW TO SAY NOTHING IN 500 WORDS

Paul Roberts

Questions for Close Reading (p. 280)

1. Roberts states the thesis at the end of paragraph six:
   "But there are some things you can do which will make your
   papers, if not throbbingly alive, at least less insufferably
   tedious than they might otherwise be."

2. The hypothetical student author of the essay on football
   seems to assume several things about the assignment: 1) that
   a student writer should try to hold an opinion that the
   professor will approve of or agree with, 2) that ending up
   with the exact number of words is one of the writer's top
   priorities, and 3) that the intelligence or vitality of the
   ideas in the essay is not very important.

3. Colorful words are those that create emotions in a reader
   or that draw a picture. Roberts calls them "dressy,"
   specific, and "loud." Colored words are those that convey
   strong favorable or unfavorable associations in addition to
   their basic meaning; another term for them is "connotative
   language." Colorless words are those so general and vague
   that they hardly have a meaning at all--words like "nice" or
   "aspect." Roberts would like student writers to be more
   attuned to the qualities of words, and he does wish students
   to beware of colorless words. He does not, however, indicate
   a blanket preference for any particular type of word.
   Instead, he suggests that a writer should decide whether
   highly colored language is appropriate for the subject
   matter, the readers, and the purpose of the writing. Writers
   should use judgment in incorporating colorful words, because,
   he writes, "it should not be supposed that the fancy word is
   always better" (36). In paragraph 43, he points out, "The
   question of whether to use loaded words or not depends on
   what is being written."

4. The author's main commandments are to avoid stating the
   obvious, try to hold an unusual position, speak in specifics,
   pare down your writing, be frank, and avoid cliches. You can
   look at the headings for sections 2 through 7 for brief
   statements of his main recommendations.

5. bromides (6): hackneyed remarks or ideas
   insufferably (6): intolerably, unbearably
   inexorably (7): relentlessly
   dissent (13): differ, disagree
   abolition (16): the act of doing away with something
   adept (20): competent
   euphemism (27): use of an inoffensive term instead of a
                       more accurate, unpleasant term
   insensible (41): unconscious

1. Roberts first presents the process by which he believes
   many students write papers--a description "exaggerated a
   little," he admits, but "not much" (5). Then he describes
   how students should write a paper; in paragraph 7 he tells
   how a student should begin, and he follows with advice on
   how to choose words and edit one's writing. The reader can
   compare the two processes and see how much more valid is the
   one Roberts recommends. The description of "how to say
   nothing" is presented for our information and amusement and
   to lay the groundwork for the discussion of how to say
   something interesting in a composition. This process is
   intended to be directional and instructive.

2. Writing to the reader directly as "you" helps Roberts
   establish a personal, friendly rapport with the students he
   intends as his audience. Most students will say that they
   come away from the essay with an image of Roberts as an
   understanding and warm teacher; he seems to speak directly to
   their concerns and to anticipate their reactions: "Well, you
   may ask, what can you do about it?" (6). He comes across as
   someone who knows them and knows how they think, and, most
   important, respects them while still urging them to improve
   their work. You might want to point out that the headings
   are in the imperative, as if preceded by "You should...."

3. The tone is warm, human, almost playful at times; but it
   is also a tone of frankness and directness. The informality
   and humanness result from a number of different techniques.
   Addressing the reader directly as "you" is one; in addition,
   Roberts uses colloquial language: "This was still funny
   during the War of 1812, but it has sort of lost its edge
   since then" (13). He has a surprising, sometimes sardonic,
   way of putting things: "All subjects, except sex, are dull
   until somebody makes them interesting" (6). He enjoys
   overstatement, just for effect, as when he provides possible
   specifics for a paper on college football (15). The sense of
   directness results from the author's frequent use of short
   sentences: "Then you go to the heart of the matter" (9), and
   from his willingness to expand on his points, provide
   examples, and give specific directions: "Don't say....Say..."
   (18). The tone is extremely effective; in fact, it may be
   the only tone possible for conveying this complex information
   about a high-level ability like writing to an audience of
   potentially hostile college students.

4. Yes, Roberts does follow his own advice. His starting
   recommendation that students seek out unpopular, uncommon, or
   hard-to defend topics and points of view for their
   compositions is itself an example of "avoiding the obvious
   content" and "taking the less usual side." Roberts also
   "avoids the obvious content" by choosing to speak in a
   personal, informal tone, instead of the typical teacherly
   authoritarian tone most students (and teachers) would expect.
   He certainly "slips out of abstraction," using numerous
   examples of weak or potentially successful topics, sentences,
   phrases, and images. Paragraph 21, for example, illustrates
   his use of specifics. The essay is quite lengthy, and so it
   may not be obvious that Roberts has "gotten rid of obvious
   padding." Yet, he does not repeat himself and is certainly
   not guilty of "circling warily around" his ideas (22).
   Rather, as he recommends in this section, he conscientiously
   illustrates and proves his points; see paragraphs 17 and 18
   for examples of how he states his idea and then develops it
   rather than "pads" it. Roberts "calls a fool a fool" by
   directly confronting the inanities of the typical student
   composition: "All bloodless, five hundred words dripping out
   of nothing..." (5) "insufferably tedious..."(6). In fact,

his portrait of the hypothetical student writer clearly reveals the folly of the student's writing process (3-4). Finally, students will have a hard time finding any cliches or euphemisms in Roberts' writing; some may cite his use of familiar expressions, such as "you're off" (3), "good ripe stuff" (3), "the brink of lunacy" (7), and "a general wringing of the hands." These are not really "pat expressions" in the sense that Roberts means, but familiar phrases used in a new context or in an interesting way. They do not "stand like a wall between the writer and thought"; rather, they are colloquialisms that help Roberts make his ideas meaningful to his audience.

BUYING A WORD PROCESSING COMPUTER

Peter McWilliams

Questions for Close Reading (p. 287)

1. McWilliams' thesis is located in paragraph 4, at the end of his intriguing introductory analogy: "In selecting a computer and selecting a religion," he writes, "I would give you the same advice: Take your time, investigate all claims carefully, don't make any hasty decisions, and remember that it must work for you."

2. Computers inspire trust and devotion, according to the author, and so he draws an analogy between picking a computer and finding a religion that is right for you. Specifically, in paragraphs 2-4, McWilliams indicates that computer owners become as emotional as religious devotees about their choices. Also, neither religious people nor computer buffs may be able to provide logical reasons for their adoration. Computer users may even harbor strange resentments against competing machines, as McWilliams admits he does (3). Finally, McWilliams suggests in paragraph 4 that a computer must suit you and your individual needs. As with religions, there is no one "best" choice for all.

3. Both the nature of the computer business and the complexity of the computer field keep computer store salespeople from being really knowledgeable. Computer experts can earn "several hundred dollars a day as consultants," McWilliams says. Since computer retail outlets pay their sales staff only minimum wage plus commissions, you can't count on these people to be experts (6). They are really just ordinary retail sales clerks eager to make a sale. Also, the author says the "Peter Principle" operates in computer stores; the really informed sales people get promoted to manager and are no longer accessible to the buyer. Salespeople who aren't very good get to stay on the sales floor (7). The incompetence of computer sales people is only to be expected, McWilliams admits, because "an ordinary human being...simply cannot keep up" with the constant innovations in "computerdom" (8).

4. McWilliams' ninth suggestion is "Take your time. Don't try to look at everything in a week..." (18), and his essay has described numerous factors that make this a good policy. Becoming an informed computer purchaser can be obstructed by

computer-users' biases (2-3) and by ignorant or ill-informed
sales staffs (6-8). In addition, rapidly changing
technologies (8) and jargon (11) can slow the buying process
down. Buyers should also, according to the author, take the
time to try out each machine, get printouts, and take notes.

5. analogy (2): an extended comparison between two things
    proselytize (2): try to convert people to one's point of view
    histrionics (4): overdramatized behavior
    rife (7): abounding
    jargon (11): specialized language of a trade or profession
    debrief (15): to take down special information from

Questions About the Writer's Craft (p. 287)

1. McWilliams does not organize his suggestions in any
    particular way. He refrains from turning his list of "hints"
    into a step-by-step description of the process of buying a
    computer, although to present the hints in a chronological
    order would be very logical. Such an organization would
    begin with the shopper's attitude (hints 9 & 10), mention
    making an appointment (hint 1), move on to how to deal with
    sales people (hints 2 & 8), describe how to test out the
    machines (hints 3-5), and end with how to decide (hints 6 &
    7).

2. Capitalizing initial letters denotes a proper noun or an
    entity deserving of special reverence. When McWilliams
    capitalizes "Knowing," "One Way," "Right Way," and "Only
    Way," he implies that computer owners believe their machines
    provide a special path to RAM -- to random access memory, or
    in other words, to computing power. The capitalizations are
    humorous, of course, as is the analogy between joining a
    religion and owning a computer.

3. McWilliams sprinkles humorous and light-hearted terms
    throughout the article, beginning with the "porcupines and
    Catholics" joke of the introductory paragraph. He makes wide
    use of colloquial language: "there is not one whit of
    difference" (3); "why on earth should they hang around a
    computer store..." (6); "computerdom" (8); "the first
    available sales person will glom onto you, and...will not be
    very willing to unglom" (10); "know enough to attempt a solo
    flight (12); "hopelessly muddled" (15); "a personal systems
    overload" (18). He also uses jaunty well-known sayings,
    sometimes with a twist: "Take the histrionics of the zealots
    with more than a few grains of salt. And save some salt for
    the journey; the road may well be slippery ahead" (4);
    "...even if his or her total knowledge of word processing can
    be written on the underside of a caraway seed" (10); "When in
    doubt about what a word or phrase means, ask. Asking may not
    do you any good, but don't be afraid to give it a try" (11);
    "Think about the unthinkable ..." (17). This unassuming tone
    helps us relax so we can learn about a technical subject, one
    which has the potential of confusing us. But the author
    keeps to short sentences, a simple vocabulary, and a
    "user-friendly" tone, encouraging us to believe we can find
    our way in the world of computers.

4. A variety of development techniques ensure that the list
    of hints remains as interesting as the rest of the article.
    The author uses examples to explain hint 4 "(Gettysburg
    Address, Pledge of Alliegance, 'Casey at the Bat,'
    anything") and hint 5. Hint 1 uses a brief process analysis
    of how sales people and customers get together. In other
    hints, McWilliams focuses on specifics, such as actions
    buyers should take: "Write down...debrief yourself...ask..."
    (hint 6), things they should say: "Why don't you take care of
    some of your other customers and come back to me later?"
    (hint 3), or questions they should ask (hint 8). Finally,
    hint 5 contains a brief personal anecdote about the many
    letters Mcwilliams wrote when he was computer shopping.

<u>COMPARISON-CONTRAST</u>

OPENING COMMENTS

     Students learn early that comparison-contrast questions
are one of the mainstays of essay exams: "Compare and/or
contrast the organizations of the Senate and the House of
Representatives"; "Discuss the similarities and/or differences
between psychotic and neurotic behavior."
     But we've found that students' familiarity with
comparison-contrast doesn't necessarily mean they know how to
structure their answers. On the contrary, students tend to
prepare helter-skelter papers that ramble every which way and
back. Yet once they are introduced to some basic strategies for
organizing a comparison-contrast discussion, their overall
ability to write clearly and logically often takes a quantum leap.
     When first using comparison-contrast, students may have
trouble organizing their thoughts. Overly concerned about making
their ideas fit into a neat symmetrical pattern, they may squeeze
their points into an artificial and awkward format. We find it
helpful to remind students that comparison-contrast is not an end
in itself but a strategy for meeting a broader rhetorical
purpose. Our reminder loosens them up a bit and encourages them
to be more flexible when organizing their papers. The student
essay "The Virtues of Growing Older" (page 301-02) helps students
appreciate that a well-organized comparison-contrast paper does
not have to follow a rigid, unyielding formula.

     We selected the readings in this chapter because, in
addition to being just plain interesting, all of them illustrate
key points about the comparison-contrast format. LeBoeuf and
Spikol deliberately develop only one side of their respective
subjects in detail. Such a skewed structure allows them to focus
on the central issue of their essays. Lurie starts her essay
with a point-by-point analysis of male and female clothing before
going on to discuss additional aspects of female dress. The
selection by Rodriguez is organized around an interesting network
of comparisons and contrasts. And Eisley uses an analogy to
dramatize a primitive similarity among earth's creatures, human
and otherwise.

JAPAN: THE PRODUCTIVITY CHALLENGE

Michael LeBoeuf

Questions for Close Reading (p. 316)

1. The thesis is located in paragraph five: "If there's one
   lesson we can learn from Japan, it's that productivity
   improvement begins with people improvement."

2. LeBoeuf points to seven factors. The first and major one
   is Japan's economic insecurity. Added to this are six
   features of Japan's unique workplace: (a) teamwork supporting
   a strong national commitment to a coordinated economy; (b) a
   high rate of personal savings and hence money for loans to
   business; (c) an obsession with knowledge; (d) a high level
   of competition in education and among businesses; (e) a
   supportive, family-style corporate culture; and (f) a highly
   trained and nurtured management force.

3. Japan seems to have overcome almost overwhelming
   conditions in its rise to international economic success.
   Its many economic disadvantages included its small size and
   high population density and its lack of resources for
   agriculture and industry. Japan also suffered great
   devastation by atomic bombs only forty years ago at the end
   of World War II and, of course, depends on the US for all of
   its national defense.

4. Attitudes about the workplace, work, and the worker are
   quite different in Japan than in the United States. For one
   thing, the Japanese treat taking a job like joining a club or
   becoming a member of a family. In paragraph 35, Le Boeuf
   describes how Japanese businesses foster company spirit by
   having workers begin the day with a company song and an
   exercise routine. Many companies have a uniform worn by all
   levels of employees, and managers often share offices to
   increase communication and a sense of togetherness.
       In addition, workers are provided total job security
   --in hard times, everyone takes a pay cut and no one is laid
   off. Typically, workers remain with a company for their entire
   lives (31). Since the goal of Japanese business is to work
   hard for the benefit of the workers and for society as a
   whole rather than just for profit (34), the Japanese feel
   personally supported by the entire economy. Also, workers at
   all levels are invited to participate in company decisions
   that affect them in any way. Individually, workers often rely
   on their company for such extensive benefits as dormitory
   housing or loans to buy houses, social clubs, and educational
   offerings.

5. longevity (2): length of human lifespan
   phenomenal (6): outstanding, remarkable
   destitute (14): living in complete poverty
   triumvirate (16): a group or association of three
   furloughed (31): laid off from work temporarily
   consensus (32): general agreement or opinion
   compile (39): to gather and organize
   counterpart (43): equivalent or corresponding items

Questions About the Writer's Craft (p. 316)

1. LeBoeuf is clearly writing for the general American
   public, an audience that knows well the facts of American
   work life and business values. As a result, LeBoeuf does not
   need to discuss the details of American business, because his

readers will make the comparisons mentally as they read about Japan. Only in the introduction, paragraphs 1-5, does the author actually refer to the economies of the Western nations.

2. Starting with the first word, "Incredible!" LeBoeuf sets a tone that is upbeat and conversational. The vocabulary of the essay is colloquial and filled with lively expressions. For example, in paragraph 8, LeBoeuf says the Japanese tell "a real hardship story" when asked about their prosperity, and in paragraph 14, he writes, "Japan works smarter.". He also reaches out to the readers by asking questions ("Does that surprise you?" (7), "Would these conditions and experiences increase your concern about American's future?" (11), and "What happens to the losers?" (29)), and by directly addressing them: "Imagine, if you would..." (10), and "Now you're beginning to understand the Japanese pangs of insecurity" (11). Throughout, the author makes sure the sentences and paragraphs are reasonably short.

3. The first three paragraphs focus on Japan's present-day success in international business, in contrast to the lesser achievements of the Western nations that had in the past ruled the world's economy. The many dramatic and surprising facts bulleted in the second paragraph serve to make us eager to read on. We are also likely to be enticed by his dramatic phrasing: "Incredible!" and "Things have changed" in paragraph one, and "Good grief, Charlie Brown!" in paragraph three.

4. The essay's opening sections contain a number of dramatic facts about Japan's productivity (2, 8, 10, 12). LeBoeuf does provide occasional solid facts, as in paragraphs 20 and 22, where he discusses how the Japanese habit of saving money has powered their economy. In paragraph 31, he provides the statistics on Japanese job security. In the rest of the essay, however, the author's examination of the Japanese workplace is based primarily on generalizations and broad assertions about conditions in Japanese corporations. There are few concrete or specific examples. Some students may feel that the essay as a whole makes a very plausible case for why Japan has been so successful economically but may wish that more proof were supplied.

MALE AND FEMALE

Alison Lurie

Questions for Close Reading (p. 325)

1. Lurie's thesis is located in the fourth paragraph: "Whether it was the first cause or not, from the earliest times one important function of clothing has been to promote erotic activity: to attract men and women to one another, thus ensuring the survival of the species....One basic purpose of costume, therefore, is to distinguish men from women." Some teachers or students may wish to refine this somewhat broad thesis; here is one possibility: "Through recent Western history, the design of women's clothing has emphasized their sexuality rather than their competence, while men's clothing has played up their power either in a physical or economic sense.'

2. Sex-typing in clothes begins early, usually while
    children are still babies. Little girls' clothing is often
    pink, the color of emotionality, or other pale colors, and is
    decorated with domestic motifs such as flowers or pets.
    Sometimes, blue is used for girls, signifying that girls will
    also serve, since blue is the color typically used for
    uniforms. The shape of girls' clothes imitates adult women's
    by emphasizing the hips, breasts and abdomen through ruffles
    and gathers (5-6). Little boys' clothes are usually in more
    "masculine" colors such as dark greens, blues and browns and
    are decorated with wild animals or vehicles. In shape, their
    clothes copy men's by being fullest at the shoulders (6).

3. The modern sack suit hides the physical characteristics
    considered important to men's social status in more
    primitive, less technological cultures: broad shoulders, slim
    waist, narrow hips, and strong legs. The padding and
    sculpting of the suit means that even men with a slight frame
    or rolls of fat look good; the suit thus standardizes men
    physically and emphasizes instead their economic and social
    attributes.

4. Corsets so severely restricted the movement of
    nineteenth-century women that only upperclass women wore
    them; these women did not have to move or work because their
    husbands could afford to hire household help. "The more
    useless and helpless a woman looked," Lurie writes, "the
    higher her presumed social status..." (11). The corset did
    more than just make women look thin and frail, however; it
    actually damaged their bodies, making them unhealthy and
    weak. It caused the back muscles to atrophy, deformed the
    ribcage, and crushed the internal organs. An uncorseted
    woman could not stand for long periods, and corseted, was
    likely to faint easily and suffer from lack of appetite and
    shallow breathing (13).

5. en masse (3): in one large group, all together
    banal (3): ordinary, unoriginal, bland
    atrophied (13): deteriorated
    debilitating (14): weakening, crippling, disabling
    tenacious (19): strong; persistent

Questions About the Writer's Craft (p. 326)

1. Lurie begins the essay with a point-by-point discussion
    of male and female clothing before going on to describe other
    features characteristic of female apparel. Each time she
    discusses some aspect of female clothing, she follows it up
    with a discussion of the corresponding aspect of male
    clothing. For example, in paragraphs 5 and 6, she points out
    the predominant clothing colors for girls and then for boys.
    Also in paragraph 6, she covers the way styles of boys' and
    then girls' clothes imitate adult dress. In paragraphs 8 and
    9, she explains how male clothes expressed first physical
    power and later social status, and then in the remaining
    paragraphs she elaborates on two themes of women's clothes
    in history, maternity and frailty.

2. In speculating how a "visitor from Mars" would view human
    clothing, the epigraph provides a lively and elegant
    introduction to the subject of the essay. It also,
    appropriately enough, points to one aspect of Lurie's theme,
    that in our culture, men's and women's clothing are
    grotesquely divergent.

3. Lurie adds some credibility to her historical discussion
of clothing by referring to specific painters (10) and novels
(12), but the bulk of her discussion is very general. She
supports her analysis of the purpose and meaning of Victorian
dress by describing the clothes--the low necks (12), the
corsets (13), and the pounds of overdresses (14)--in some
detail, but she does not otherwise provide evidence for her
interpretation of what these fashions mean. The quotation in
the concluding paragraph from Thorsten Veblen, a seminal
social and economic theorist (author of The Theory of the
Leisure Class, 1899), provides support by showing that
another analyst has examined female fashion and discovered a
plot to render women powerless.

4. Overall, Lurie's tone is objective and analytical, but
she is also open about her position on women's fashion. She
conveys her point of view in the choice of an adverb:
"More ominously, these clothes ensured the charming
ill-health of their wearers..." (12); in her use of irony:
"But then, ladies did not 'walk,' since in polite discourse
they had no legs--rather they 'glided' or 'swept' across the
floor like carpet sweepers..." (15) and "A lady might be pure
and innocent, of course, but this purity and innocence could
be preserved only by constant vigilance" (16); and in the
strong terms of her analysis in the final section: "...a
helpless, foolish, pretty woman is the ultimate object of
Conspicuous Consumption...." "The Dumb Blonde's tight satin
sheath, spike heels and long, brittle, varnished nails...make
her prestigious uselessness obvious" (18). Finally, Lurie's
last sentence is a clear condemnation of clothes that
handicap women's ability to take care of themselves.

HIGH NOON

Art Spikol

Questions for Close Reading (p. 334)

1. The first sentence suggests the main point that Spikol is
trying to make, and some students will choose it as the
thesis. However, this sentence fails to convey the
emotional impact of the Saturday matinee and the desire
Spikol has to share this delightful part of his youth with
his child. The thesis in its fullest sense is implied: "The
Saturday matinee symbolized a time of freedom, optimism,
adventure, and indulgence, which the author longs to share
again."

2. The Saturday matinees offered many enjoyments to young
Spikol: the adventure films, with their cliff-hanging endings
and innocent hinting at sex; the excitement of an audience
unified in its booing of the enemy and its cheering of heroes
(13, 14); the reenactment of battles on the way home.
Overall, "There was something unrestrained about Saturday
matinees..." he writes (19). Clearly they fulfilled his
needs for excitement and fantasy.

3. "While kids haven't changed much," Spikol writes, "the world around them has" (23). The world presents children with a much more sophisticated view of life. Today's kids watch realistic crime drama on TV, are up-to-date on current events, and are aware of hypocrisy. They can't believe in the exaggerated adventures and magical rescues that characterized the old matinees.

4. The matinee seems to embody the spirit of the era in which Spikol grew up--a time of clear and definite national values for which he does feel some nostalgia. He remembers cheering at cartoons that dramatized the fight against Hitler (13) and saluting the flag as the soldiers in the audience would do, rather than putting his hand over his heart during the national anthem (24). He points out that his feeling of total involvement in the experience was due in part to the innocence of the times: "We didn't question the flag. We didn't know it could be used to cover things up..." (24).

5. chafed (1): became impatient
   transfixed (11): rendered motionless in awe or terror
   crescendo (11): an increase in intensity and volume
   indoctrinating (13): teaching to accept certain beliefs
   substantiate (21): confirm, verify
   furlough (24): leave of absence

Questions About the Writer's Craft (p. 334)

1. Spikol interweaves his comparison of the past and the present, making a couple of switches back and forth. In paragraph 3, as he drives, Spikol talks about the past in general, and in paragraph 4, he returns to the present, providing a first description of the modern theatre he is going to visit. In paragraph 6, he moves to a specific description of his childhood movie-going experiences and returns to the present in paragraph 20. He briefly returns again to the past in paragraph 24, and then moves to a concluding paragraph. Spikol is very direct about his transitions from one era to another, sometimes taking a whole sentence to point out he is making a shift: "But first, let me tell you about 1944..." (6); "I had hoped to find it alive and well at the Parkwood Manor..." (20).

2. "High Noon" refers, first of all, to the fact that matinees are shown at noon. In addition, the movie High Noon--which Spikol never actually mentions in the essay-- is a famous symbol of a showdown between the forces of good and evil. Here, in this essay, the showdown is between the past and the present, or rather, between Spikol's memory of the matinees and the current trend in Saturday afternoon entertainment. Clearly, the matinee era has been shot down by the modern world. Also, the film High Noon typifies the drama, suspense and simplified morality of the old-fashioned movies that he loved so much: "an era in which you could always tell the good guys from the bad, the right causes from the wrong..." (26).

3. Spikol can count on his audience to understand what today's movie theatres and matinees are like, so he doesn't need to describe that side of his comparison in much depth. He does not want to remind us what a modern matinee is like; he wants to reveal what it lacks. Also, he goes beyond objectively comparing or analyzing the two eras; he wishes to use the contrast to explore his memories and his values.

4. "Th-th-tha-that's all, folks!" is Spikol's way of bidding goodbye to the era of matinees and to the innocence, gaiety, and charm it possessed.

WORKERS

Richard Rodriguez

Questions for Close Reading (p. 343)

1. The thesis of "Workers" is implied. One way of
   expressing it might be: "A summer of hard physical labor is
   not enough to teach a young middle-class college graduate
   what it is like to be poor or Mexican, or what it means to
   make construction work one's livelihood."

2. Rodriguez writes that desire for the job "uncoiled" in
   him as soon as he heard about it. This surprised him,
   although he was in need of money at the time (1). In the
   weeks leading up to the job, he realized that he felt
   challenged to learn, after four years in college, what it was
   like to work hard physically (3). In doing so, he would
   overcome his father's scorn that the young Rodriguez did not
   know what "real work" was. He was also intrigued by the
   thought of the sensations that would come from working in the
   open, under the sun, and by the chance to become "like a
   bracero" (4).

3. Very quickly the contrast between the "real laborers" and
   Rodriguez becomes apparent to him. He is only flirting with
   being a construction worker before going on to graduate
   school, while the other men do construction work for a
   living. Unlike them, he appreciates the sheer physicality of
   the work. When the older men try to show him how to shovel
   efficiently, so as not to waste energy or strain his back,
   he feels resistant to their instruction. "I liked the way my
   body felt sore at the end of the day," he writes (7).

4. Rodriguez comes to recognize he has little in common with
   los pobres, the Mexican aliens who occasionally cut
   trees and haul debris, although at first he seems to think
   there might be some natural kinship between himself and them.
   After all, they are Mexicans, like Rodriguez's parents; he
   is "physically indistinguishable" from them (17). He even
   speaks a rudimentary Spanish and can communicate with them in
   their native tongue. They treat him as an outsider,
   however, and he realizes he is of a different world. He
   earns a wage, while they are paid "for the job," as if they
   had no individual identities. They stay apart from the
   regular workers, work with little rest, converse rarely, and
   are powerless to change their situation. "They lack a public
   identity....They depend upon the relative good will or
   fairness of their employers each day" (19). In addition,
   they must be submissive to retain the good will of employers;
   they are vulnerable in a way Rodriguez will never be.
   Rodriguez has a self-determined future ahead of him, the
   result of his college education. He says he can "act as a
   public person--able to defend my interests, to unionize, to
   petition, to speak up--to challenge and demand" (18). He
   states the difference philosophically at the end of paragraph
   17: "What made me different from them was an attitude of
   mind, my imagination of myself."

5. menial (1): servile, subservient
   skepticism (4): doubt
   luxuriating (5): wallowing in pleasure
   diversity (9): variety, quality of difference
   ludicrous (16): laughable, absurd
   nouveau riche (18): the newly rich
   pathos (20): quality of arousing pity or sorrow

1. The author is more like the American construction workers
   than the Mexican laborers; the details provided in paragraph
   9 make his similarity to the Americans clear. He is able to
   find other workers that he can relate to, because some, like
   himself, have college degrees; one is an abstract painter in
   the off-hours. Also, these workers accept him, while the
   Mexicans do not. "I felt easy, pleased by the knowledge that
   I was casually accepted, my presence taken for granted by men
   (exotics) who worked with their hands," he writes (9).
   Other details reveal that these workers are "middle-class
   Americans," like himself, who follow football, vacation in
   Las Vegas, and consider the merits of different campers,
   presumably in view of purchasing one (9). The details about
   the Mexicans, on the other hand, show them to be alienated,
   silent, and submissive (11, 15).

2. There are five narrative segments in the piece: the
   stories of how Rodriguez heard about the job and how he came
   to take it (1-3, 4); the story of the older workers teaching
   him how to shovel (6-8); the narrative of his Spanish
   conversation with the Mexican workers (12-15); and the
   description of how the boss pays the Mexicans (16). The
   anecdotes about the Mexicans come last because the experience
   of working with them generates Rodriguez's most important
   point--that he will never be like them, that his attempt to
   recover a more elemental, ancestral self was a failure. The
   anecdotes occur in chronological order at first: hearing
   about a job, getting it, and learning to do the work. In
   putting the Mexican anecdotes last, Rodriguez switches to
   emphatic organization.

3. Rodriguez mixes in a few Spanish words to suggest his
   origins. In terms of the theme, these foreign words express
   the author's uncertain identity: as a highly educated
   American of Mexican descent, he feels neither like an
   "all-American worker" nor like the Mexican laborers; the
   Spanish terms convey his middle position between the two
   groups. Also, Spanish in general, and the words he chooses
   in particular, such as
   bracero, tie into his craving to vindicate himself in
   terms of his father's value system, which celebrates "real work."

4. The subjective descriptions of how it feels to do hard
   physical work occur mostly in paragraph 5. Students will
   probably find two phrases especially striking: "my chest
   silky with sweat in the breeze" and "a nervous spark of pain
   would...burn like an ember in the thick of my shoulder."

THE BROWN WASPS

Loren Eiseley

<u>Questions</u> <u>for</u> <u>Close</u> <u>Reading</u> (p. 353)

1. It is through a special place, or a memory of that place,
    that people identify and know themselves and find a center to
    their lives. In paragraph 8, Eiseley writes, "We cling to a
    time and a place because without them man is lost, not only
    man, but life." In the next paragraph, he continues, "It is
    as though all living creatures, and particularly the more
    intelligent, can survive only by fixing or transforming a bit
    of time into space or by securing a bit of space with its
    objects immortalized and made permanent in time."

2. Eiseley has seen old wasps, living on into midwinter,
    return to find refuge in abandoned hives for a short time
    before dying. Likewise, he sees old men, poor and homeless,
    seek out the comfort of a familiar landmark, the city train
    station, before succumbing to death. Eiseley realizes he has
    also clung throughout the years to a familiar place by
    returning to it over and over again in his memory; now, as an
    old man, he revisits this place, the yard of his childhood
    home, where he and his father planted a tree. He calls
    himself "one of the brown wasps" because he too seeks the
    past, its comfort and familiarity, as he grows older and more
    aware of death.

3. Since its construction will destroy the minute and
    delicate nature that thrives in the empty field, Eiseley
    opposes the new store. It symbolizes progress ("Here a man
    was advancing"), but a futile kind of progress, for it
    destroys only to succumb in turn to the destructive forces of
    time and nature ("but in a few years his plaster and bricks
    would be disappearing once more into the insatiable maw of
    the clover").

4. In his mind, Eiseley had lived with the image of the
    special cottonwood tree all his life, and so he answers the
    boy in the present tense. Even though the beloved tree has
    been long dead, his response, "I do," affirms the importance
    and permanence of memory, which outlasts places.

5. <u>oblivion</u> (1): forgetfulness
    <u>vaporous</u> (8): mist-like
    <u>guises</u> (9): forms, appearances
    <u>tentatively</u> (10): uncertainly, experimentally
    <u>essence</u> (16): fundamental nature or most important quality
    <u>stanchions</u> (17): vertical posts or poles
    <u>pneumatic</u> (21): run by compressed air
    <u>vista</u> (25): view

<u>Questions</u> <u>About</u> <u>the</u> <u>Writer's</u> <u>Craft</u> (p. 353)

1. The similarity between wasps and people is the focus of
    the essay. Eiseley emphasizes the way both humble creatures
    and humans feel an allegiance to a particular place from
    their past; all are vulnerable to the ravages of change.

2. Students may choose to discuss any number of descriptive
    details in the essay. These include the portrayal of
    different kinds of creatures, such as the slug and the "huge,
    blackbelted bee" in paragraph 10, the mice (11), and the
    pigeons (17-22), and also visually powerful descriptions of
    places, such as the barnlike El station (17), the grassy

field (10), and the fern pots on his carpeted floor (13).
Eiseley's attention to detail evokes the livingness of the
creatures and the sheer physicality of every moment of our
lives. These descriptions thus reinforce his theme that all
creatures rely on places for their sense of a center to their
lives.

3. Note the words Eiseley's father spoke during the
    planting of the tree: "We'll plant a tree here, son, and
    we're not going to move anymore. And when you're an old, old
    man you can sit under it and think how we planted it here,
    you and me, together." Throughout Eiseley's life, the tree
    has symbolized his father's promise of security and
    permanence, a promise broken by the forces of change. To the
    mature man, the tree represents the indelible longing for
    roots and a home. Other symbols of the "homing instinct"
    include the wasps, the mouse, and the pigeons; the store
    construction and the demolition of the El symbolize change
    and destructive progress.

4. Most students will find such creatures abhorrent,
    frightening, or, at the least, trivial. By letting such
    animals dramatize the tendency to long for the past, Eiseley
    puts our humanness in a new perspective. Through these
    symbols we can find a renewed link to all of existence.
    Also, in showing that this need for place occurs in creatures
    of all kinds, Eiseley renders his theme all the more
    powerful.

<u>CAUSE-EFFECT</u>

OPENING COMMENTS

        Along with comparison-contrast, cause-effect writing
(often called causal analysis) is frequently required of college
students--especially in exam situations ("Analyze the causes of
the country's spiraling divorce rate"; "Discuss the impact of the
revised tax laws on middle income families.") And since students
can't deny that an ability to write sound causal analyses will
serve them well, they are generally eager to tackle this
rhetorical pattern.
        Not surprisingly, though, many students run into problems
with their analyses. Although they enjoy the intellectual
challenge of tracing causes and effects, they sometimes stop at
the obvious, overly-concerned as they are about getting closure
on an issue.
        We've found a classroom activity that helps counteract
this urge to oversimplify. Here's what we do. We put on the
board a broad, noncontroversial statement (for example, "In the
United States, many people work hard to keep physically fit").
Then we ask students to take five minutes--we time them and
announce when the time is up--to brainstorm the reasons <u>why</u>
(causes) people are so involved in physical fitness. Then we ask
students to spend another five minutes brainstorming the
<u>consequences</u> (effects) of this concern with physical
fitness. Next, we put students in pairs and then in groups of
four; each time they exchange, first, their causes and then their
effects. As you'd expect, this activity generates a good deal of
energy, and we hear a number of comments such as, "That's
interesting. I never thought of that." Such a reaction is
precisely what we hoped for. The activity sensitizes students to
the complexity of cause-effect relationships and encourages them
to dig deeply and not settle for the obvious.

        For this chapter, we chose professional selections which
dramatize the power of causal analysis to make the reader think.
The pieces by Gallup and Schwartz, both of them speculative as
well as persuasive in intent, raise some interesting questions
about current trends in family life and communication technology.
Farb and Thomas explore complex causal chains, encouraging
readers to examine their own attitudes and experiences. And
students will be challenged by and may even disagree--as many
sociologists have--with the analogy at the heart of Wolfe's
causal analysis.

THE FALTERING FAMILY

George Gallup

Questions for Close Reading (p. 384)

1. Gallup presents his main idea as an answer to the
    question in paragraph 5: "What are the pressures that have
    emerged in the past twenty years that cause long-standing
    family bonds to be broken?" He cites as the main general
    pressure "a major change that occurred in the
    mid-sixties,...an explicit widespread rejection of the common
    values about sexual and family relationships that most
    Americans in the past had held up as an ideal" (6). The rest
    of the essay goes on to discuss the nature of this rejection.

2. According to Gallup, the change in American attitudes to
    marriage and family came about through four groups of
    pressures, reflected in the headings that divide the
    selection: alternate lifestyles, sexual morality, the
    economy, and grassroots feminist philosophy.

3. Gallup reports a wide range of new styles of couples: gay
    people who wish to be considered married, heterosexual
    couples who live together without marriage, and experiments
    in communal living and open marriage. New styles of
    parenting include single people who adopt or bear children
    out of wedlock, artificial insemination, and the increasingly
    popular option to remain childless.

4. Many different factors have brought about the movement of
    women into the workforce, according to the author. The
    economy is one major factor, for unemployment has been a
    significant and persistent social problem in our nation.
    When husbands lose their jobs, both spouses start
    job-hunting, and often, the author says, it is the wife who
    succeeds. In addition, the cost of raising children is
    exhorbitantly high, often requiring a second income. Besides
    the economic pressures, Gallup has located an attitude change
    among the younger generation; its members are very
    materialistic, and both young women and young men view a
    career as the means to enjoying life (29). A second area of
    attitude change is the "filtering down" of feminist
    philosophy to the "grassroots" level, the author says.
    Nowadays, most young women say they want to attend college
    and pursue a career (32, 35). Gallup believes that these
    factors represent permanent changes in our country; the
    economy seems to remain a continual pressure on our lives,
    and attitude changes on the part of young people and at the
    "grassroots" level are implicitly ones that will endure.

5. explicit (6): readily observable
    proliferation (9): rapid increase
    inseminated (13): impregnated
    salvage (38): rescue
    ambivalent (39): the state of having mixed feelings

Questions About the Writer's Craft (p. 384)

1. The word "pressures" suggests forces acting upon our
    society to bring about change; "pressures" seem to act in a
    more general, less specifiable way than "causes," and thus,
    by using this term, Gallup avoids claiming to have discovered
    scientifically provable causes of broad behavior and attitude
    changes in the United States. He also makes no claim that

this list of pressures is exhaustive--there may be other
forces at work as well. Finally, students may point out that
the term "pressures" has negative connotations, unlike the
term "causes," which is more neutral. "Pressures" suggests
negative causes or causes that produce negative effects.

2. The selection begins with an introductory anecdote about
children's widespread fear of divorce (1-2). Readers are
likely to feel sentimental about children and concern or even
pity for their precarious situation in possibly deteriorating
families.   Then, in paragraph 4, Gallup uses statistics to
prove that "family-oriented concerns" are among the five
major problems facing the United States. Gallup thus uses
the techniques of anecdote and statistics to make the reader
more receptive to the idea that American family life is
changing for the worse. The data contained in the article
does confirm that the family is changing, but really focuses
on alternative life styles. In actuality, divorce is not the
subject of the article. In fact, Gallup does not mention
divorce until near the end, in paragraphs 34 and 38.
Thematically, then, the introduction is not well related to
the subject matter of the essay; it seems to function only to
attract the reader's interest and to create concern about the
general subject of the American family.

3. Statistics support some of the points about alternative
lifestyles (16), sexual morality (19, 21), the economy (28),
and feminism (32, 37-39); many of these statistics are
derived, as you might expect, from Gallup polls. Other, more
general statements are also clearly based on Gallup's own
research (25-26, 32, 37). The author also makes widespread
use of facts drawn from other sources, which he is careful to
cite (10, 13, 16, 21, 22, 28, 32). There are also, however,
a large number of comments based on unnamed surveys or other
research. For example, in paragraph 15, he says, "Most
surveys show...." and "...there are periodic reports of...";
in paragraph 27, he writes, "Economists agree..." In these
and other paragraphs, it is difficult to know where he is
getting his ideas. See also paragraphs 11, 29, and 31 for
other examples of unattributed information. Overall, Gallup
demonstrates that these alternative lifestyles and value
changes do exist in the U.S. today; he does not, however,
provide proof that these changes have damaged the family or
America's children.

4. The essay has a very objective format; it is highly
structured, using headings for each major concept and bullets
to separate and emphasize points (10-16, 21-22). Also, the
frequent references to the sources of information give the
reader the impression of a well-researched, authoritative
report on American lifestyle today. However, there are
numerous hints that Gallup himself is not totally neutral
regarding his subject.   He uses many terms that show he is
biased toward the traditional-style family. For example, in
paragraph 5 he refers to the breaking of "long-standing
family bonds," and in paragraph 6, to the "common values...
that most Americans in the past had held up as an ideal." In
the section on Alternative Lifestyles, he writes about the
"typical American family who...lived happily ever after," a
model one was supposed to follow to gain "full" or "normal"
membership in society. Likewise, some of his descriptions of
alternatives to the standard marriage and family model are
somewhat pejorative. He says that people living other
lifestyles were "always considered somewhat odd" (8), for
example, and in summing up his section on Sexual Morality,
contrasts "traditional priorities" such as marriage and
monogamy with "the desire for unrestrained sex." Finally,
the title of the selection, "The Faltering Family," also
suggests the author regrets the changes he is chronicling.

IN OTHER WORDS

Peter Farb

Questions for Close Reading (p. 392)

1. Farb's thesis is located at the end of paragraph 3:
    "...only recently has it been shown scientifically that all
    speakers constantly detect and interpret such [body language]
    cues also, even though they do not realize it."

2. The phenomenon of an animal interpreting body language
    and coordinating its behavior accordingly is a perfectly
    normal one, and not "phenomenal" or exceptional at all,
    according to the article. All animals and people interpret
    such cues; Farb's examples include horses, rats, naive
    humans, psychologists conducting experiments, and children.

3. The rat experiment tested whether or not biased
    experimenters obtained results from their trained rats that
    coordinated with their biases. The subjects, or "rats," were
    really the "experimenters," the people training the rats, not
    the rats themselves.

4. The Harvard psychologists proved that preconceptions in
    the minds of teachers about students do cause them to send
    non-verbal body language signals that affect the students'
    performance levels. Secretly believing some students to be
    "spurters," the teachers subtly treated these students
    differently, and, indeed, these students tested higher at the
    end of the school year. The teachers were the real subjects
    or "rats" in this experiment, for it was their behavior that
    was being studied.

5. unwittingly (2): unknowingly
    linguistics (5): study of language
    blatantly (10): conspicuously

Questions About the Writer's Craft (p. 392)

1. On the game show, the simple cause of runs of right
    answers   is that one partner "reads the mind" of the other
    or just takes "lucky guesses." Researchers studying tapes of
    such shows were able to identify body language cues that
    assisted the guessing partner to come up with the right
    answer.
         In psychological experiments using human subjects,
    results are supposed to indicate the truth or falsity of a
    hypothesis; results that run according to the hypothesis can
    be explained, in other words, by the hypothesis being true.
    Actually, researchers believe that some experimenters
    inadvertently manipulate the subjects by their body language
    at the time they explain the experiment to the participants,
    and thus they influence the subjects to produce results that
    confirm the desired hypothesis.
         In the maze experiment, the simple explanation would be
    the one which the rat-trainers believed, that some rats were
    smarter and inherently more skilled than others. However,
    all the rats were actually identical, and the variation in
    success in maze-running coordinated with the preconceptions
    of the trainers. This indicated that the true cause of the
    results was the bias in the trainers' minds that caused them
    to treat the supposedly intelligent rats with special care.

In the California classroom, the simple explanation for some students excelling after one year of schooling would be that they were smarter or had received extra help; neither possibility was true, . The actual cause of their high achievements was the subtle body language cues they had received from their teachers telling them that they were especially smart.

2. Farb's first example, that of Clever Hans, is intriguing and would appeal to non-scientists; he uses it to arouse the interest of the general reader and provide a clear instance of how powerful body language is. The second example, that of the game show contestants, is also easy to comprehend and relates the concept of body language to our contemporary experience. Using these two examples at the start, the author maintains reader interest while introducing a scientific concept. The essay uses an emphatic organization pattern, moving from the least important example to the most convincing, the scientific research. The essay climaxes with the experiment performed on students and teachers, in which the results concretely affected the lives of young children. This experiment has wide-ranging social impact and ends the essay forcefully.

3. Farb's discussions of the everyday examples of body language, Hans and the game shows, contain few qualifiers. Examine, for example, the positive tone in the last sentence of paragraph 2 and in the thesis statement; the third sentence in paragraph 4 does contain a qualifier: "It turned out that _sometimes_ the contestants also gave body signals that were much more informative than the verbal clues." As Farb moves into discussing scientific research, qualifiers appear more often: "...trained psychological experimenters also unintentionally flash body signals which are _sometimes_ detected by the test subjects--and which _may_ distort the results of experiments" (5); "...the sex of the experimenter, for example, _can_ influence the responses of subjects" (5); "male experimenters smiled _about_ six times as often with female subjects..." (5); "The answer is that it _often_ does" (6); "...the subjects could predict _almost_ _immediately_..." (6); "..._usually_ he is indignant when told that his experiment was biased" (7); "...the experimenters' expectations about the results of the experiment _actually_ _result_ in those expectations coming true" (7); "...the black and brown children _probably_ will do poorly..." (9) "...some or all of these things _must_ _have_ communicated that the teachers expected improved performance..." (12). The essay shows a slight decrease in qualifiers in the discussion of the school experiment, coordinating with Farb's more emphatic tone in this section.

4. Farb does have a serious point to make in his last paragraph: that teachers need to stop negatively influencing the performance of disdadvantaged students. He believes we need to retrain teachers rather than remediate students who have been influenced to fail. His way of putting this point is ironic, showing his anger about how destructive body language cues can be if unchecked.

OH ROTTEN GOTHAM--SLIDING DOWN INTO THE BEHAVIORAL SINK

Tom Wolfe

Questions for Close Reading (p. 402)

1. Wolfe's thesis is implied. You might state it as:
    "Overcrowding of humans is likely to take its toll, just as
    it has been proven to destroy the health of animals and their
    societies." Another way of stating it could be: "Research on
    animals shows overcrowding is destructive to animal societies
    and can even cause death; similar effects may result when
    humans are overcrowded."

2. Dr. Hall is using the word "waste" ironically, to mean
    that he really doesn't consider the vaulted ceilings of Grand
    Central Station to be a waste of space at all. In fact, he
    obviously thinks the ceilings are the only thing that makes
    the station at all bearable. He also recognizes, however,
    that in modern cities, space is valuable and expensive, and
    high ceilings are likely to be a thing of the past. Wolfe
    probably includes the remark because he agrees that the
    future is likely to hold increased overcrowding.

3. Although he lives and teaches in Chicago, Dr. Hall
    travels east to study the classic examples of overcrowding in
    New York. (Wolfe provides details that indicate Hall lives a
    "relaxed, civilized" and certainly not overcrowded life in a
    "high-ceilinged townhouse" in Chicago.) John Calhoun is, like
    Hall, an ethologist; Wolfe reports on his research on the
    effects of overcrowding on rats because it may relate to how
    overcrowding affects humans. Just as, according to Hall,
    overcrowding has turned New York into a "behavioral sink,"
    Calhoun's experiments created a "behavioral sink" among rats.

4. The male rats reacted by becoming overly competitive,
    aggressive, and sexually deviant. The females became
    ravaged, ill, and uninterested in nurturing their young.
    Hall's observations in Grand Central Station seem to focus
    primarily on typical commuters--mostly male, white,
    middle-class professionals commuting from their suburban
    homes. Later in the essay, Wolfe openly refers to the "white
    humans" (22) and describes a hypothetical stressed-out person
    as a "work-a-daddy human animal" (23).

5. autistic (1): showing signs of autism, a mental disorder
                   characterized by withdrawal
    chancred (1): having chancres, skin sores often
                  associated with venereal disease
    etiolate (4): pale and sickly
    effluvia (8): offensive smells
    sebaceous (8): pertaining to the body's fat
    ethologist (12): person who studies animal behavior
    satyrism (15): excessive, uncontrollable sexual desire
    andrenocortical (21): pertaining to the adrenal glands'
                          outer layer, which secretes hormones

Questions About the Writer's Craft (p. 402)

1. The causal chain begins with stress--such as Wolfe
    describes in paragraphs 2 through 6: the stresses of
    overcrowding, rushing and darting about, and excess noise.
    The stress causes the adrenal glands to swell (6), and
    deviant behavior results (18). Ultimately, the enlarged
    adrenals cause death (21, 22). Wolfe actually suggests the
    outlines of this chain in the first paragraph: "Overcrowding
    gets the adrenalin going, and the adrenalin gets them queer,
    autistic, sadistic, barren, batty, sloppy, hot-in-the-pants,
    chancred-on-the-flanckers, leering, puling, numb--the usual
    in New York, in other words, and God knows what else."

Wolfe organizes the essay by first establishing that the overcrowded humans in Grand Central are just like animals (2, 4). He then examines research on overcrowded rats that shows the effects of overcrowding on animal behavior and on Sika deer that shows the effects on health.

2. The first shift of topic occurs in paragraph 12, where Wolfe moves from Dr. Hall's study of human behavior to discuss the rat experiments conducted by John Calhoun; to prepare the reader for the discussion of Calhoun's work, he uses the question "Why?" and a brief statement about how much animal research is being done. For the most part, however, Wolfe moves from topic to topic with very little warning to the reader. For example, in paragraph 20, he moves quickly from Calhoun's work to "the classic study of die-off" done by John J. Christian. The return to Grand Central Station, the scene of Hall's research, comes suddenly in paragraph 22, and in paragraph 24 Wolfe pulls in the research done by Rene Dubos using only a brief transitional sentence: "One of the people whose work Dr. Hall is interested in on this score is Rene Dubos at the Rockefeller Institute."

3. Exaggeration marks the style of this essay from the very first paragraph: "Thousands of my fellow New Yorkers short-circuiting themselves into hot little twitching death balls with jolts of their own adrenalin.... the adrenalin gets them queer, autistic, sadistic, barren, batty, sloppy, hot-in-the-pants, chancred-on-the-flankers, leering, puling, numb--the usual in New York...." Other exaggerated descriptions occur in paragraph 8: "nice big fluffy fumes of human sweat, urine, effluvia, and sebaceous secretions"; paragraph 10: "and in all of them the adrenals grow..."; paragraph 23: "noises up to the boil-a-brain decibel level" and "the adrenals ooze to a halt, the size of eggplants in July." Paragraph 22 contains a quotation from Dr. Hall that is also an exaggeration: "There is enough acid flowing in the stomachs in every car to dissolve the rails underneath." Throughout the essay, Wolfe confines hyperbole to his descriptions of frantic commuters and the stress-filled city around them; his descriptions of the research on rats and deer is detailed and colorful, but does not use exaggerated language. Some readers may accuse Wolfe of distortion because of the exaggerated way he describes the human subjects of Hall's study; most of the time, we expect writing about science to stick to the plain unembellished facts. However, Wolfe is not writing a scientific paper. Rather, he uses vibrant comparisons and hyperbole to make reading about science enjoyable. While on the one hand, he seems not to take the dangers of NY life very seriously, on the other, the extreme vividness of his descriptions may sway readers to agree that NY is a behavioral sink.

4. Wolfe's tone, like that of Dr. Hall, is sarcastic and detached. He seems to be mocking New Yorkers as they scurry around in the behavioral sink. When he discusses the results of research on overcrowding, Wolfe becomes a bit more restrained and serious. Students may debate whether the tone is appropriate to the subject. Strictly speaking, scientific subjects demand a neutral tone; here, Wolfe's lightness makes the essay very readable, but we may be shocked by the clash of the subject and the tone. In addition, the vividness of the descriptions may persuade a reader that our society is indeed endangered by overcrowding. In other words, Wolfe's style and tone may be more convincing than just a neutral discussion of the ethological evidence. Finally, Wolfe's refusal to be alarmed at the "population collapse" and imminent "die-off" in New York suggests that he and Dr. Hall are like the aristocrat rats, safe from the decline in the behavioral sink because they live in a safer, more luxurious level of society.

COMMUNICATION IN THE YEAR 2000

Tony Schwartz

Questions for Close Reading (p. 411)

1. Schwartz states his thesis in the first sentence of the article: "During these last two decades of the century, a broad range of communication technologies will develop and change how many of us work, learn, and use leisure time."

2. Current laws, Schwartz says, are designed to keep the various communication industries -- computer, telephone and television -- from overlapping. Hybrid communication systems, such as those using cable TV for two-way mesages between broadcaster and viewer, represent a serious regulatory problem (or "nightmare") because they are based on the mixing of the different communication media.

3. While Schwartz points out numerous obstacles to the growth of new communication systems in paragraph 2, he believes that the odds are in favor of their proliferation. There are three factors that convince him of this: 1) electronic systems start out expensive, but tend to get cheaper and cheaper as they are perfected; 2) the success of these systems will come through their appeal to special-interest groups ("narrowcasting"), not to audiences in the millions; 3) the two-way participative nature of these new systems will make them attractive to many people.

4. The numerous changes in American life likely to be created by interactive communication services are listed in paragraphs 17 to 21. They include the loss of influence by the major TV networks and the use of the TV to receive a much wider range of information and entertainment (17); the transformation of the home into a workplace linked to offices through various technological means (18); the increased use of technology to conduct interpersonal relationships between individuals (19); the improved accessibility of information to the general public (20); the possibility of instant feedback from the public to politicians and legislators (21).

5. hybrids (2): combinations
   moguls (2): very powerful people
   viable (3): workable
   feasible (5): possible
   telemetry (14): transmitting information by wire or radio

Questions About the Writer's Craft (p. 412)

1. Schwartz has much information to relay about the new communication systems that are appearing in our country, but he also wishes to make predictions about likely future developments. His double purpose is to inform and to speculate on the possibilities.

2. The essay consists of four sections: the first covers the reasons why new communication systems will grow (3); the second discusses the variety and kinds of new technologies (4-9); the third suggests uses for these new technologies (10-16); and the fourth presents the possible effects these changes could have on our lives (17-21). The lead-off sentence of the first paragraph in each of these sections eases the reader into the new phase of the essay. Paragraph 3 begins with a direct statement of where the essay is going to move: "However, three characteristics of the new communication systems suggest that they may indeed arrive in

our homes and offices." The opening phrase of paragraph 4 directs our attention to the new types of communication by suggesting a look at the most familiar: "Perhaps the best way to think about these new communication services is to begin with the telephone." The third section devotes a whole paragraph to transition, and uses focusing questions to direct us toward new uses of technologies: "What kinds of services, entertainment, and information do people want, and what will they buy, watch, and listen to?" (10). Finally, the first sentence of the fourth section summarizes the concept just discussed, that new communication services might become common in the American home and workplace, and leads into the discussion of effects: "If new communication services (or a significant portion of them) make their way into the average home and office, the so-called effects may be quite far-reaching (17)."

3. Schwartz uses an objective, serious tone throughout the essay; there are no touches of levity or even any descriptive flourishes in the body of the article. The author remains very businesslike and analytical. This tone works well with his subject; since he is speculating on possibilities, his analytic even tone helps the reader accept him as a credible authority whose ideas are well thought out and probably valid.

4. Despite his neutral tone, Schwartz comes across as interested and suportive of the new technologies and the possibilities they present. Most likely, he restricts his discussion of problems to the end because he does not want to detract from his main theme. Once he does move to the possible problems, however, he focuses on one example--the likely change in our government. He notes that technology has already determined one important aspect of the President's job--the short time-span in which a decision would have to be made in case of a missile attack (23). Schwartz's language in this paragraph is very dramatic. He speaks of technology as a "second god" in order to drive home the point that these electronic systems which we have created now have the power to change or recreate our world. The "second god" image forces us to recognize the critical importance of technology today.

THE HEALTH CARE SYSTEM

Lewis Thomas

Questions For Close Reading (p. 418)

1. You can find the thesis in paragraphs 8 and 9: "As a people, we have become obsessed with Health. There is something fundamentally, radically unhealthy about all this."

2. Much of the advertising on radio and television concerns health, diets, illnesses and remedies. Also, the plots of many television shows, not only those set in hospitals, focus on illness and disease. For these reasons, Thomas considers the electronic media to be a "huge marketplace" (3) dominated by the theme of health improvement. He clearly finds this situation a negative influence on the American public.

3. Thomas offers as support the huge and ever-escalating
    dollar amounts we in the US spend each year for health care
    services (1). He also cites the prevalence of illness and
    disease on TV and radio shows, in advertising, and in
    publishing (4-5); our expenditures to improve our environment
    by eliminating health-damaging pollutants (6); and the
    national obsession with such exercises as jogging, tennis,
    and bicycling (7) to prove that we are driven by the goal of
    improving our health. Notice that Thomas supports this idea
    inductively, in that he presents his evidence first
    (paragraphs 4-7), and then, in paragraphs 8 and 9, tells us
    the conclusion he draws from this evidence.

4. To prove that we are healthier than in the past, Thomas
    points to our low national death rate--under 1% in 1976--and
    our high life expectancy, 72 years and rising. He adds that
    many previously devastating illnesses, such as TB and
    pneumonia, have been brought under control, and that our most
    common illnesses today are not life-threatening.

5. <u>malodorousness</u> (4): condition of having a bad smell
    <u>furuncles</u> (4): boils
    <u>surrogate</u> (4): substitute
    <u>anomie</u> (11): feelings of personal disorder and alienation
    <u>contingencies</u> (14): future emergencies

<u>Questions</u> <u>About</u> <u>the</u> <u>Writer's</u> <u>Craft</u> (p. 418)

    1. According to Thomas, the overpromotion of health care and
    health aids by the media and in society in general has caused
    our obsession with the state of our health. He cites this
    cause in paragraph 11: "...it can only be accounted for by as
    a manifestation of spontaneous, undirected, societal
    <u>propaganda</u>"; the effect is summed up in the thesis
    (8-9), and paragraph 10 presents a short discussion of the
    psychological consequences of this propaganda. The early
    paragraphs of the essay describe the concrete effects of this
    obsession: our huge outlay of money for health care (1-2),
    the dependence of several other major industries (the media,
    publishing, environmental protection) on our desire to be
    healthier, and our preoccupation with sports and fitness.
        You might want to point out that Thomas identifies a causal
    chain in this essay: the propaganda about health and illness
    causes us to be obsessed, which causes us to jog, take
    vitamins, and read diet books, which causes us to be so
    occupied that we haven't got time or energy to deal with
    "other, considerably more urgent problems" (15).
        Thomas supports this cause-effect relationship in a broad
    way, by general reference to Americans' behavior. He uses
    facts only to support the point that our health-care industry
    costs a great deal; the essay lacks any additional specific
    illustrations or other proof of his assertions. The author
    even hedges the cause-effect relationship somewhat by using
    qualifiers: "...perhaps it can only be accounted for..."
    (11). In addition, Thomas seems to use the media as both a
    cause of our national obsession with health (11) and as an
    effect (4-6); while undoubtedly our national attitude towards
    health is very complex in its origins, many students may find
    his use of the media as both cause and effect quite
    illogical.

2. Paragraph 12 serves to refute the notion that Americans
    are unhealthy; by stuffing it with statistics and other
    information on our longevity, Thomas wishes to impress us
    with the validity of his position. Its length represents the
    author's strong conviction that we are, undeniably, a
    healthy people.

3. Obvious examples of overstatement include: "The
   transformation of our environment ...costing rather more than
   the moon" (6); Tennis has become...a rigorous discipline, a
   form of collective physiotherapy" (7); "Jogging is done by
   swarms of people...in underpants" (7); "Bicycles are cures"
   (7); "We live in danger of falling apart at any
   moment...always in need of surveillance and propping up.
   Without the...health-care system, we would fall in our
   tracks" (10); "In the end, we would all become doctors..."
   (13). Other, perhaps less apparent, exaggerations occur in
   the early paragraphs about the media: "The television and
   radio industry... feeds on Health..." (4); "the food industry
   plays the role of a surrogate physician..." (4); and "The
   publishing industry...seems to be kept alive by Health..."
   (5).
       Many of these overstatements verge on the comic ("joggers
   in underpants..."); overall, Thomas' tone is sarcastic. Many
   students will enjoy his irreverence, but others may find that
   the exaggerations somewhat undermine Thomas's credibility.
   While the author means to mock our over-concern with health
   by using an exaggerated tone, for some people this strategy
   may boomerang: it may create the impression that Americans
   are not really so obsessed with health, since Thomas had to
   so exaggerate to make his point.

4. Capitalization is reserved for proper nouns. By
   capitalizing the "H" in health, Thomas acts as if health were
   more than a concept or an abstract noun; he treats it as if
   it were an entity in itself, an institution or perhaps a
   being, such as a god to be worshipped.

OPENING COMMENTS

In high school and certainly in college, students
frequently answer questions that ask for definitions: ("Define
'mitosis'; "Explain what 'divestiture' means.") Even so, we hold
off discussing definition as a method of development until the
last quarter of the course. Here's our thinking.
Since extended definitions can be developed through a
variety of rhetorical patterns, students need to be familiar with
those patterns before they can prepare a well-supported
definition essay. At the very least, they need to know how to
marshall well-chosen examples so that their definitions can be
grounded in specifics. Similarly, the comparison-contrast format
can show students how to go about organizing a definition by
negation. And process analysis, explaining how something works,
is often critical when developing a definition. Once students
feel comfortable with these and other rhetorical strategies, they
can approach definition essays with confidence, knowing that they
have a repertoire of techniques to draw upon.

For this chapter, we selected readings that illustrate a
variety of approaches for writing definition essays. Touching
upon a wide range of topics, the pieces show how definition can
explain difficult-to-understand scientific concepts. The
selections also demonstrate that the pattern can be used to
challenge the meaning we attach to common everyday words. We
often start with Cole since she mixes a number of strategies
(examples, facts, personal anecdotes) to develop her definition
of entropy. We like Chase and Winn's essays because they offer
compelling proof that definition by negation can be effective
when advancing a personal interpretation of a term. Finally, the
pieces by Mencken and Syfers make an interesting pair. Using
satire to define, respectively, a "politician" and a "wife," both
essays provide new insights and spark heated discussion.

ENTROPY

K.C. Cole

Questions for Close Reading (p. 440)

1. Cole's thesis is located at the start of paragraph 3,
    after her two-paragraph introduction: "Disorder, alas, is
    the natural order of things in the universe."

2. Entropy is unique in being irreversible; most physical
    properties "work both ways" (3). In nature, things fall
    apart and decay, and they do not naturally reverse and come

together. The "arrow of time" image helps us understand that entropy occurs in relation to time; as time passes, disorder naturally accompanies it. Entropy is the "arrow" also in the sense that it is the weapon time uses to destroy things.

3. The creation of life is the ordering of the particles of matter into a living thing, be it a plant or a person, and so represents the major contradiction to entropy. Such creation, however, requires energy in the form of nutrients such as, for a plant, soil, sun, carbon and water, and for a person, "oxygen and pizza and milk" (9). Cole's other examples show that countering entropy does generally require energy in the form of physical work, the work of cleaning up chlidren's rooms, painting old buildings (4), or maintaining skill at flute-playing (12). Cole points out that creating order and countering entropy require energy whose expenditure causes an increase in entropy in another part of the system; she uses as an example our society's creation of electricity by burning oil and coal, only to produce smog.

4. Entropy is "no laughing matter" because it is inevitable, and it operates not only in nature, but in society as well. There are "always so many more paths toward disorder than toward order," Cole writes (14), and unless we are diligent, entropy will get the better of us individually and societally. This ever-present threat of disorder is especially distressing in the area of social institutions and international events. Cole belives that the ultimate randomness of entropy endangers us--the "lack of common purpose in the world" (15) threatens to create more and more disorder.

5. futility (1): sense of uselessness
    dissipated (6): scattered, spread out
    buffeted (7): hit, slapped, pushed
    tepid (7): lukewarm
    atrophied: 12): deteriorated

Questions About the Writer's Craft (p. 441)

1. Entropy is a phenomenon we surely have noted--rooms getting messy, wood rotting, metal rusting--but it is not likely we have understood it to have a name or be a "principle" of the universe. So Cole's definition is informative about this scientific law. In explaining the need for energy to counteract entropy (10-12) and in relating entropy to societal and world events, however, Cole adopts a persuasive tone. In paragraph 16, she cautions, "Friendships and families and economies all fall apart unless we constantly make an effort to keep them working and well oiled." Clearly, she is making a pitch for us all to work harder at keeping order in our world.

2. Speaking like a common person with average concerns, such as her refrigerator breaking and her tooth needing root canal work, Cole encouages a reader to follow her into a discussion of entropy as an explanation for these ordinary problems. She achieves friendly, almost breezy tone by using the first person, contractions, short sentences, and colloquialisms such as "lukewarm mess" (5), "to get ourselves together" (10), and "the catch is" (10). The question in the second paragraph is another example of her personable, casual tone.

3. These terms are blunt and jarring and carry an intense impact. Throughout the essay, Cole uses these emotional words to keep us aware of the personal dimensions of entropy. While entropy is a scientific concept, she wants us to

understand that it also pertains to our personal lives, and has effects we can respond to emotionally. Some other similar terms are "unnerving" (4), "lost and buffeted" (7), "distressed," "afraid," "terrified," and "upset" (15).

4. This sentence pattern emphasizes contrasts--it contains an inherent opposition between the elements of the first and second half. Cole may find this pattern useful because she is trying to dramatize the effects of entropy and convince us to counteract its power as best we can. The first example compares the two "roads" to disorder and creation, finding one downhill, the other uphill. The second example compares ways to do "a sloppy job" and a "good one." Other examples occur throughout the essay: "Once it's created, it can never be destroyed (3)"; "When my refrigerator was working, it kept all the cold air ordered in one part of the kitchen....Once it broke down the warm and cold mixed into a lukewarm mess that allowed my butter to melt..." (5); "Though combating entropy is possible, it also has its price"; "That's why it seems so hard to get ourselves together, so easy to let ourselves fall apart" (10); "...creating order in one corner of the universe always creates more disorder somewhere else"; "We create ordered energy from oil and coal at the price of the entropy of smog" (11); "The chances that it will wander in the direction of my refrigerator at any point are exactly 50-50. The chances that it will wander away from my refrigerator are also 50-50" (13); "...there are always so many more paths toward disorder than toward order. There are so many more different ways to do a sloppy job than a good one, so many more ways to make a mess than to clean it up" (14); "The more pieces in the puzzle, the harder it is to put back together once order is disturbed" (17).

A VERY PRIVATE UTOPIA

Stuart Chase

Questions for Close Reading (p. 451)

1. At the end of paragraph 4, the author tells us specifically that the essay is going to "delimit the kind of life one personally would like to live." This sentence serves as the focusing sentence for the whole essay; since it does not express the content, students may decide that the thesis is implied: "People should strive to make their society one in which they can truly feel alive, rather than deadened by the trivial, the ugly, the cruel, and the mechanical."

2. Chase describes his private Utopia so that he can explain what he believes modern industrial civilization should strive to be. He finds that most critics of American culture point out only the shortcomings and fail to make known their standards for a happy society. Mumford's book is one example of this tendency to criticize without recommending alternatives. Chase wishes to make known "what he is for."

3. The first list contains the conditions that Chase finds deadening, those that reduce him "to merely existing." The second list provides the conditions that make him feel alive.

After sharing these private images of "the good life," Chase goes on to explain the kind of community he would build to support such a lifestyle for himself and others. He thus broadens the scope of his comments from his specific desires to a scheme for society as a whole.

4. Chase's list reflects only what would make him thrive, but he designs his Utopia to include whatever might bring happiness to others. For example, in paragraph 20, he says he will have a church if someone wants it; members of his Utopia can play different games than those that attract him, work at whatever they find fun, and roam through the country as nomads if they wish.

5. indefatigable (1): tireless
   corpus (5): body
   foibles (7): slight frailty in character
   sanguinary (8): bloody
   infallible (9): incapable of making a mistake
   plethora (14): overabundance
   indigenous (17): native
   spurious (21): false, unreal
   nirvana (23): state of complete spiritual bliss

Questions About the Writer's Craft (p. 451)

1. Students may find much to agree with in Chase's list of deadening experiences; many will read this list with heads nodding, murmuring, "Right!" to themselves. (You might want to solicit the items they particularly identify with in order to begin the discussion of how this negative list affects them.) In venting his complaints first, Chase gets his readers on his side; also, they are more likely to comprehend his positive suggestions after he has revealed what he finds so negative about our society.

2. Although Chase claims that most of the time he is "dead," he must have written this essay during a period of great vitality. It fairly bursts with passion and expressiveness; rather than conveying the deadness of his life, it demonstrates just how alive he can be. Given this zestful tone, we might assume that he is exaggerating the extent of his usual "deadness."

3. Chase is extremely clear about moving to a new phase of his discussion; his writing amounts to a model of strong directive transitions. In paragraphs 3 and 10, for example, he asks questions to focus our attention on the points he is going to make. He introduces his lists with very straightforward comments in paragraphs 7 and 8. As he moves to discuss the qualities of his ideal society, he uses enumeration (paragraphs 11-14, 18).

4. Chase defuses objections by calling his Utopia a "crude" "preliminary definition" (20). He indicates in several places in the essay that it is only a provisional version of a better society. For example, in paragraph 9, he says it would be "ridiculous" to assume that his lists would apply to all. In the next paragraph, he emphasizes the relativity of the positive and negative, depending on our moods and health. Later in the the essay, in paragraphs 20-21, he invites people to change and adapt his Utopia so that it fits their needs as well. He concludes by humbly stating that his essay is "a feeble and absurd beginning" to the search for a better life. Given the number of disclaimers, it seems that Chase counted on his audience being skeptical of and resistant to his Utopia.

WHY I WANT A WIFE

Judy Syfers

Questions for Close Reading (p. 455)

1. Syfers states explicitly in paragraph 2 that she would
    like a wife: "As I thought about him while I was ironing one
    evening, it suddenly occurred to me that I, too, would like
    to have a wife." A fuller statement of the thesis, however,
    would summarize her reasons and might read: "A wife is
    desirable, even for a woman, because a 'wife' can be defined
    as a person who does all the work no one wants to do, who
    keeps track of all details, and who does not ask for anything
    in return."

2. The visit of an old male friend, recently divorced,
    prompted her stream of thought about the usefulness of wives.
    This ex-husband turned up free and in search of a new wife,
    while his ex-wife wound up with the full-time care of their
    child. The husband's callousness and the obvious unfairness
    of the divorce ties in to Syfer's desire to have, rather than
    be, a wife.

3. Wives efface themselves and devote all their time to
    furthering such goals of their husbands as putting them
    through school (3) and entertaining their business guests
    (6). They minister to the every need of their children (4),
    avoid complaining (5), and are sexually compliant (7).

4. While a wife devotes herself to the needs of the family,
    the husband is free to please himself. He expects her to
    listen to his insights, but refuses to listen to her
    complaints (5). He chooses whom they entertain (6) and
    insists she understand he needs an occasional night out alone
    (6). He even maintains that he may have to violate monogamy
    to satisfy his sexual needs (7), while she must not disturb
    his peace of mind by having any affairs of her own. The
    final statement of the difference between the spouses occurs
    in paragraph 8, where the husband asserts the right to trade
    in his wife, leaving the children with her, to take on a
    "fresh new wife."

5. nurturant (3): giving affectionate care and attention
    replenished (6): refilled
    entail (7): involve
    adherence (7): loyalty

Questions About the Writer's Craft (p. 455)

1. Syfers initially amuses us with the absurdity of a woman
    claiming she wants a wife, but gradually her insistence
    conveys resentment. Throughout the rest of the article, she
    seems sarcastic, even bitter, about the injustices wives put
    up with. The tone effectively conveys the stress,
    frustration, and indignity of the wife's role.

2. Repeating the phrase "I want a wife" over and over drums
    the author's desire insistently into our minds. At first, it
    conveys her desperation for relief from the burdens and
    frustrations of being a wife herself. As she continues to
    repeat this phrase, however, she seems increasingly assertive
    and demanding, perhaps as demanding as husbands tend to be of
    their wives. Her style is in fact so direct and forceful
    that we might find it "unfeminine." These repetitions
    make the speaker of the essay seem like the kind of person
    who would want a slave-like marriage partner.

3. While at first the order of points might seem random, actually they progress in emphatic order from the basic duties of housework and childcare to various social duties and then to the wife's sexual duties. As the list goes on, the husband is revealed as increasingly self-centered and inconsiderate. At the end, the speaker names the final outrage, that he wants the right to change wives if he feels like it.

4. The essay's development consists of details piled on; Syfers fairly overwhelms the reader with the list of a wife's duties. She never summarizes or provides a direct definition of a wife.

THE POLITICIAN

H.L. Mencken

Questions for Close Reading (p. 462)

1. The first paragraph indicates Mencken's point of view about his subject: Politicians "seldom if ever get there [public office] by merit alone, at least in democratic states." Mencken continues, "They are chosen normally for quite different reasons, the chief of which is simply their power to impress and enchant the intellectually underprivileged." Later in the essay, he puts it another way: "In brief, they will divest themselves of their characters...and become simply candidates for office, bent only on collaring votes" (5).

2. Mencken reports that he has found most politicians to be honest, knowledgeable, and realistic. Once campaigning starts, however, these "enterprising" and "charming" (3) people learn that only by pleasing the ignorant public can votes be won, and so they start to make unkeepable promises and utter all sorts of nonsense.

3. The voters are at fault, because they vote only for candidates who talk nonsense (6). Truth, Mencken says, is equivalent to a headache for most people, and good sense makes them uncomfortable, like a tight collar (2).

4. Mencken avoids naming names because he is defining a type, the politician. He also wants to avoid abandoning his journalistic neutrality and appearing to take sides. "I am not in politics," he says (3). However, as journalists, he and the other reporter seem to be privy to the personal side of candidates, a side they do not report to the public. While he attacks politicians in general, he protects them individually.

5. candid (1): frank, honest
   austere (1): grave, somber
   adamantine (2): uncompromising
   dipsomaniac (2): alcoholic
   sagacity (4): wisdom
   demagogy (4): the practice of gaining power by appealing
                 to people's emotions and prejudices
   succor (5): assist
   interlocutor (7): person participating in a conversation

1. Mencken builds his definition by first describing the
   process by which a "larval statesman" (2) turns into a
   "rascal" (5). Paragraph 2 is also an example of causal
   analysis. In paragraphs 6 and 7, he provides a specific,
   although unnamed, example of this transformation. The
   concluding paragraph provides a brief narrative of a specific
   conversation Mencken held with a candidate. Mencken relies
   on anecdote and his credibility as a social critic rather
   than offer hard evidence for his allegations.

2. "The intellectually underprivileged" (1), "customers"
   (2), and "huge packs of morons...wallowing in the pap..." are
   some of the insults that Mencken applies to the average
   American voter. He doesn't spare the candidates, of course,
   saying they are all either "amateurs" or "professionals" in
   the "science" of demagogy" (4) and "rascals" (6).

3. Mencken's opening sentence presents him as a reasonable
   and humane critic. He humorously blames himself for
   harboring unreasonable expectations of politicians. He also
   builds his credibility by letting us know he is personally
   acquainted with numerous candidates. More subtly, he uses
   phrases that convey certainty and encourage us to side with
   him: "plainly enough," "obviously," and "anyone must realize
   who reflects..." (1) He is clearly aiming his essay at those
   who do reflect, those who are above the ignorant masses.

4. A radio crooner, a movie actor, and a bishop (1) comprise
   the first juxtaposition, which suggests that all these are in
   show business and sets the stage for Mencken's implication
   that politicians are, too. In the third paragraph, he lumps
   together burglars, child-stealers, and Darwinians. All three
   are thieves, he indicates, of diamonds, daughters, and
   liberty, respectively. In differentiating politicians from
   these he may be proposing that they are not so low as common
   thieves nor so dangerous as biological determinists. In
   paragraph five, he pairs "curing warts" and "paying off the
   national debt," hinting that both amount to mere
   charlatanism. In paragraph 6, he claims voters throw
   "flowers, hot dogs and five-cent cigars" at popular
   candidates, thus mixing the expected (flowers) with the
   unlikely to convey the absurdity of the people's adulation.
   You might want to point out that many of these juxtapositions
   mix different levels of language (the formal and the
   colloquial) in addition to mixing images.

TV ADDICTION

Marie Winn

Questions for Close Reading (p. 467)

1. Winn's thesis is implied; one way of putting it might be:
   "If addiction is defined as a pleasurable activity or
   substance which demands repetition and which destroys normal
   creative life, watching television is an addiction."

2. Gardening and reading mysteries are called "addictions"
   by people who over-indulge in them or "pursue [them] with

unusual intensity," in Winn's words; they are, however, truly pleasure-giving and often productive activities, not destructive to a normal balanced life. For Winn, the "essence of any serious addiction" is the search for a special feeling of pleasure, for a "high" unavailable any other way (3).

3. Winn's initial definition of addiction in paragraphs 3 and 4 sets out this dynamic of pleasure that creates a need for repetition. Addicts, of whatever type, find life without the addictive pleasure empty and incomplete. Winn writes, "The addict craves an experience and yet he is never really satisfied. The organism may be temporarily sated, but soon it begins to crave again" (4). In the light of this, the television addict's failure to be sated with the pleasure of TV is not really contradictory.

4. Winn's list of creative alternatives runs the gamut of hobbies: reading, gardening, sewing, crocheting, and playing games (10). She also mentions conversing (10) and communicating (11) as important alternatives to TV watching.

5. wryly (1): ironically
inchoately (7: vaguely, partially
ruefully (10): regretfully
adverse (11): detrimental
satiation (12): satisfaction, fulfillment

Questions About the Writer's Craft (p. 468)

1. Such common, everyday pursuits as gardening, reading mysteries, and eating cookies are not addictions, Winn says, although we may jokingly refer to them as such. Winn begins by explaining why most such ordinary pursuits are not actually addictions, because her goal in this essay is to persuade us that the term addiction is reasonably applied to one particular common, everyday habit, viewing television. Once she has established the harmlessness of most of these everyday obsessions, she focuses on why habitual TV watching is different--and dangerous.

2. Winn develops the two definitions in parallel fashion. In defining addiction in general in paragraphs 3 through 5, she establishes three main characteristics of the problem: the pursuit of pleasure, the compulsion to repeat, and the stunting of normal life and personal growth. In her analysis of TV addiction, Winn follows the same pattern of points, first showing that TV is pleasurable, then that it becomes an insatiable need, and finally that excess TV viewing destroys a healthy life. By making this point-by-point analysis, Winn provides argumentative support for her thesis.

3. This confession of addiction comes from a member of a group we might at first assume to be impervious to the pleasures of TV: a college instructor, an intelligent person with vital intellectual interests. That such a person testifies to the hypnotizing power of television makes Winn's thesis more credible. Also, the quotation's dramatic, almost frightening, image of how dreadful this addiction can be is certain to make an impression on the reader: "I feel sapped, will-less, enervated....the strength goes out of my arms...."

4. Winn's discussion of how to define addiction is very analytical; it covers each aspect of it point-by-point. Then Winn relates TV viewing to each of these points. In developing her essay this way, Winn wants to make sure that we see TV watching as not merely analogous to an addiction, but as an actual "diagnosable" psychological addiction in itself.

DIVISION-CLASSIFICATION

OPENING COMMENTS

We confess. We always feel slightly uneasy about
teaching division-classification as a distinct rhetorical
pattern. After all, the logic at the core of division-
classification comes into play a number of times during the
writing process. For example, when students generate thoughts
during the prewriting stage, when they outline their ideas, when
they prepare process analyses, they instinctively draw upon the
ordering principles characteristic of division-classification.
But even though many students automatically use
division-classification, we nevertheless teach it as a discrete
method of development. We do so because the pattern helps
students understand the demands of logical analysis.

We usually cover division-classification near the end of
the semester, though it could be discussed much earlier. Our
thinking is that the analytic rigor demanded by the
division-classification process prepares students for their final
and perhaps most challenging assignment--the argumentation-
persuasion essay.

Working with division-classification causes two problems
for students. First, they become confused about the difference
between division and classification. They think they're
classifying when they're dividing and dividing when they're
classifying. On pages 474-75, we state as succinctly as we can
the difference between these two related but separate processes:
Division involves taking a <u>single</u> <u>unit</u> or <u>concept</u>,
<u>breaking</u> <u>the</u> <u>unit</u> <u>down</u> into its parts, and then analyzing the
connection among the parts and between the parts and the whole.
Classification <u>brings</u> <u>two</u> <u>or</u> <u>more</u> <u>related</u> <u>items</u> <u>together</u> and
categorizes them according to type or kind.

Second, some students view division-classification as
a pointless exercise designed by overparticular composition
teachers. When they learn that they've been using
division-classification all along (when brainstorming, when
outlining, and so on), they begin to understand that
division-classification is a valuable tool for logical analysis.
In this connection, the student essay "The Truth About College
Professors" (pages 484-86) will provide the class with a good
laugh (perhaps even at your expense) and help students see how to
use classification to make a point.

This chapter's professional essays show how
division-classification can help writers analyze many different
subjects. Barry's humorous yet biting mock script for a TV
newscast uses division to depict the mindlessness of local news
programs. Zinsser, Hilifiker, and McClintock classify,
respectively, college students' pressures, physicians' errors,
and Madison Avenue's propaganda techniques. In-class discussion
of these last three pieces can help you focus on the authors' use
of overlapping categories and will certainly raise provocative
questions about contemporary value systems. And Morris' essay,
which examines a wide range of social and not-so-social human
behaviors, illustrates the use of transitional cues between the
categories and sub-categories of a subject.

IN DEPTH, BUT SHALLOWLY

Dave Barry

Questions for Close Reading (p. 495)

1. The thesis appears in the first paragraph: "If you want
    to take your mind off the troubles of the real world, you
    should watch local TV news shows. I know of no better way to
    escape reality...."

2. Barry finds news shows have a typical cast: a male anchor, a
    female co-anchor (both with alliterating names), a reporter
    from a significant minority group (read "Black"), a likable
    sports reporter, and a joking weatherman with a pretentious
    degree. All the "personalities" are white males, except for
    the token female and black. (During the show, another
    reporter who is possibly female ("Terri Tompkins") appears.)
    Barry includes a "drummer" facetiously, to underscore the
    fact that local news often resembles entertainment shows
    (such as The Tonight Show, for example) more than news.

3. On local news, coverage is extended to any event with a
    strong visual component: accidents and fires, primarily.
    Barry writes that for local TV, news is "anything that you
    can take a picture of, especially if a local TV News
    Personality can stand in front of it." More abstract
    issues, such as the economy, don't receive much coverage
    because there's no obvious visual to put on the screen.

4. Child abuse and rollerskating receive special attention
    on this broadcast, but the reporters provide no real
    information on either subject. In her special report,
    co-anchor Snape limits herself to emoting and stating the
    obvious (most child abuse occurs in houses); the segment on
    skating consists only of footage of Terri Tompkins skating
    outside the studio.

Questions About the Writer's Craft (p. 495)

1. Barry's purpose is to show that local news is thoroughly
    inane--and so he scripts a whole show, segment by segment.
    This way, he can demonstrate that each supposedly
    "informative" portion is actually deficient in substance and
    overloaded with trivia, emotionality, and chitchat. These
    criticisms suggest that local news shows need to be less
    entertaining; they should provide information and analysis,
    and they should pay less attention to cuteness and visual
    effects.

2. Like the producers of TV news, Barry recognizes that the
    general public finds analysis a bore--and so he makes his
    point in an entertaining, humorous way. Using a spoof rather
    than a serious critique may also be Barry's way of suggesting
    that local TV news is so farcical it is not worth treating
    seriously.

3. Seeing TV news compared to heavy drinking gives the
    reader a jolt. The piece begins with criticism of local news,
    but this comparison at the end of the paragraph is outrageous
    and irreverent. It sets the tone of absurdity that dominates
    the essay, while also conveying the strength of Barry's
    convictions on this subject.

4.   Westbrook and his colleagues use the phrase "actual color
     film" no less than nine times, in paragraphs 5, 15, 16, 20,
     and 26. Such repetitions indicate how stuffed with useless
     verbiage and filler the broadcast is; also, the repetitions
     show the cast members constantly patting themselves on the
     back for the most simple accomplishments. Other repeated
     phrases are "On-the-Spot Action Eyewitness News," used seven
     times in paragraphs 4, 5, 6, 14, 20, and 30, and "On-the-Spot
     Reporter," used in paragraphs 5 and 19; "three-county area"
     appears eight times in paragraphs 12, 15, 17, 19, 21, 23, and
     26.

COLLEGE PRESSURES

William Zinsser

Questions for Close Reading (p. 505)

1.   Zinsser states his thesis explicitly in paragraph 7, at
     the end of his long introduction to the essay: "I see four
     kinds of pressure working on college students today: economic
     pressure, parental pressure, peer pressure, and self-induced
     pressure."

2.   The pressures come from the economy, parents, peers, and
     the individual students themselves. The notes to Carlos
     reveal the emotional harm students suffer as a result of
     these pressures, and in the rest of the essay, Zinsser
     explains that these pressures cause more than just
     psychological pain; they also inhibit students' intellectual
     growth and narrow the range of their college activities. He
     points out such harms as excessive studying and overexertion
     (27-29), rigid career choices and half-hearted concurrence
     with parental wishes (19-22), lack of experimentation (33),
     failure to get a liberal education (11), retreat from
     creativity (22), rivalry between friends (24), and deemphasis
     of extracurricular activities (36). As Carlos Hortas puts
     it, "Violence is being done to the undergraduate experience"
     (32).

3.   The four pressures that Zinsser cites do not exist
     independently, but are "intertwined" or related to each
     other. In discussing the "intertwining" of pressures,
     Zinsser divides the four pressures into two pairs. In
     paragraph 14, he says, "Along with economic pressure goes
     parental pressure. Inevitably, the two are deeply
     intertwined." He means that economic pressure affects
     students as parental pressure, because the parents pay the
     bills, for the most part, and often expect compliance in the
     form of high grades and a practical major. Zinsser
     introduces the other pair of pressures in paragraph 23:
     "Peer pressure and self-induced pressure are also
     intertwined...." The example of two roommates, each of whom
     suffered feelings of academic inferiority in relation to the
     other, points out that such peer pressure is often created or
     imagined by students who feel a great inner compulsion to
     excel.

4.   Students must "break the circles in which they are
     trapped," Zinsser writes (31). As individuals, they need to
     stop following their parents' dreams and reacting to their

classmates' fears. They must start to believe in their own
uniqueness and their own power to achieve a future right for
them (31). Zinsser quotes the dean Carlos Hortas, who
agrees that students "ought to take chances" (33). Specific
remedies are implied rather than stated directly; they
include joining extracurricular activities (36-7), risking
experimentation and failure (5), going ahead with creative
aspirations (22), sampling a wide variety of courses (11),
and taking time to relax and enjoy life (25).

5. privy (3): made knowledgeable to secret or special
                information
    venerated (6): worshipped, highly regarded
    exhorted (13): urged
    tenacity (15): perseverence, persistence
    vacillates (22): wavers
    furtively (22): secretly
    circuitous (40): roundabout, indirect

Questions About the Writer's Craft (p. 506)

1. Zinsser's pairing of the pressures on college students is
    quite logical and reflects the reality of students' lives.
    The first pair, economic and parental pressure, is external.
    These two pressures come from society at large and from
    parents. The other two pressures, mass competitiveness among
    peers and an inner obssession to excel, affect students
    psychologically. These pairs make the essay's argument
    easier to grasp, because they reduce the four points to two
    larger ones; also, the pairing of pressures helps the reader
    to understand how the pressures interlock and overwhelm
    today's students.

2. The pressures on students to drive themselves hard and
    have a practical goal are essentially causes, and the
    desperate feelings and compulsive behaviors of the students
    are the results or effects of these causes. The essay can
    thus be viewed as an example of a causal analysis as
    well as of division- classification. Zinsser uses a pattern
    of first discussing effects and then showing the causes. For
    example, paragraphs 8 and 9 focus on some effects of the
    economic pressures: the beliefs that grades and decisions
    about majors determine a student's life; the economic causes
    underlying these beliefs are revealed in paragraphs 12 and
    13. The next section follows this same pattern; paragraphs
    15 to 19 present a student reluctantly pursuing an M.D., and
    paragraphs 20 and 21 discuss the causes of such pragmatic
    decisions. In the section discussing peer pressure and inner
    pressures, Zinsser again begins with an anecdote
    demonstrating the effects of the pressures (29) and follows
    with an analysis of the causes. Paragraph 27 presents a
    causal chain in which the effects become causes of still
    further effects.

3. The students' notes to Carlos make an engrossing lead-in
    to the essay. They capture our attention because they are so
    colloquial and yet so terse, so packed with emotion and
    occasional black humor. Also, these notes focus our
    attention on the theme, that many students today experience
    college as agony because of the pressures they are under.
    The self-portraits painted by these notes show that students
    are not, as a reader might imagine, carefree or rebellious,
    driven to irresponsible frivolity or to serious challenges of
    society, but rather overwhelmed and frightened victims. On
    the positive side, they do maintain a sense of humor ("Hey
    Carlos, good news! I've got mononucleosis."), struggle
    valiantly with their problems ("I stayed up all night ... &
    am typing.... P.S. I'm going to the dentist. Pain is pretty
    bad.") and are not afraid to reach out for help.

4. Such an exaggerated description of what students want
    shows sarcasm on the part of the author; the description here
    is almost a put-down of students who succumb to the idea that
    they must map out their lives completely. Other examples
    occur in paragraphs 1 ("Who are these wretched
    supplicants,...seeking such miracles of postponement and
    balm?"), 9 ("The transcript has become a sacred document, the
    passport to security. How one appears on paper is more
    important than how one appears in person"), and 15 ("They go
    off to their labs as if they were going to the dentist").
    This ironic tone is found mainly in the beginning of the
    essay, as Zinsser is still luring his readers into the
    article. As he examines the intertwining of pressures, he
    drops the hyperbole and uses a more analytic tone.

MAKING MEDICAL MISTAKES

David Hilfiker

Questions for Close Reading (p. 519)

1. In paragraph 20, the author directly states his main
    point that "We [doctors] are not prepared for our mistakes
    and we don't know how to cope with them when they occur."

2. Four urine tests for pregnancy all returned negative
    results, providing seemingly overwhelming evidence that the
    fetus had died. As a result, Dr. Hilfiker ignored the other
    signs of Mrs. Daily's pregnancy--her enlarged uterus and the
    lack of a spontaneous miscarriage. He believed an ultrasound
    test would be too expensive and too inconvenient for the
    Dailys, since it would require a drive to Duluth, over one
    hundred miles away.

3. A "failure of will" results when a doctor knows the right
    thing to do but is too exhausted or distracted to do it. To
    Hilfiker, this seems the worst kind of mistake, because the
    doctor has the capacity and knowledge to make the correct
    decision. After such a failure, a doctor may feel very
    guilty, believing that with more "will power," the fatigue or
    pressure might have been overcome and the proper decision
    made.

4. Dr. Hilfiker sought to discover the reasons for his
    mistakes. After the death of the Dailys' baby, for example,
    he "placed several frantic phone calls" (13) and discussed
    the case with his colleagues (24) in order to determine what
    had happened. He also felt guilty and angry (24) and
    questioned his own competence (43). Hilfiker points out that
    he has little idea how other doctors deal with their
    mistakes, because physicians in general avoid any discussion
    of their errors (46). In general, medical schools do not
    prepare their students for the fact that errors occur
    "regularly" in the practice of medicine (44-45).

5. alleviate (6): relieve, lighten
    rationale (15): reasons
    thwarted (23): frustrated
    angina (33): angina pectoris, a disease marked by brief,
                    sharp chest pains caused by lack of oxygen to
                    the heart
    rationalize (35): justify
    culpability (48): guilt
    absolution (49): pardon

1. Hilfiker divides mistakes into those resulting from a
   lack of knowledge (28), a lack of technical skill (30),
   carelessness (31), a failure of judgment (32), and a failure
   of will (32). In addition, some mistakes are so complex they
   defy classification (36). The principle of division is the
   causes of the mistakes.

2. The beginning narrative is engrossing and dramatic; it
   provides a strong human-interest hook for the reader and
   alerts us to the life-and-death seriousness of the author's
   topic. Hilfiker adopts a candid, personal tone to tell this
   story. Most students will see him as human and fallible, yet
   admirable in his honesty, courage, and concern to face the
   tragedy of medical mistakes squarely.

3. Hilfiker provides numerous examples of medical
   mistakes, both his own and those of others. In the second
   half of the essay, he analyzes the process by which such
   mistakes come to be made and also the processes that have led
   the medical profession to ignore them for so long.

4. In analyzing the reasons for a particular medical
   mistake, the author often uses a question to demonstrate his
   dilemma: could he have saved the patient by doing something
   differently? Such questions appear in paragraphs 33, 35,
   41, 42, 43, and 50. Where Hilfiker discusses complex
   failures whose cause cannot be truly known, unanswerable
   questions abound (41 and 42). The questions in the essay are
   rhetorical, for the most part.

PROPAGANDA TECHNIQUES IN TODAY'S ADVERTISING

Ann McClintock

Questions for Close Reading (p. 529)

1. McClintock's thesis is located at the end of the first
   paragraph: "Advertisers lean heavily on propaganda to sell
   their products, whether the 'products' are a brand of
   toothpaste, a candidate for office, or a particular political
   viewpoint."

2. Propaganda is the "systematic effort to influence
   people's opinions, to win them over to a certain view or
   side" (2) in terms of product choices, political candidates,
   or social concerns. Many people associate propaganda solely
   with the subversive campaigns of foreign powers or with the
   spreading of outrageous lies to an unwitting, innocent
   populace. But actually, propaganda is all around us; it is
   used by all the special interests that vie for our attention,
   our dollars, and our votes. American advertising is pervaded
   with propaganda in its attempt to sell us commercial
   products, and our political climate suffers from blizzard
   after blizzard of propaganda before each election.

3. Advertisers use "weasel words" to "stack the cards" and
    distort facts so that their products appear superior. Weasel
    words are words that say more than they mean and suggest more
    value than they actually denote. For example, an ad might
    say a shampoo "helps control dandruff," but we might
    understand this to mean that it cures dandruff (19).

4. Consumers should be aware of propaganda techniques so
    they can resist the appeal of ads that distort the truth or
    pull at our emotions. Only when we can separate the actual
    message and evaluate it for ourselves are we doing the hard
    work of clear thinking: "analyzing a claim, researching the
    facts, examining both sides of an issue, using logic to see
    the flaws in an argument" (23).

5. <u>seduced</u> (1): enticed, entranced; mislead
    <u>warmongers</u> (5): people who attempt to start wars
    <u>elitist</u> (17: belonging to an exclusive or privileged group

Questions About the Writer's Craft (p. 529)

1. The definition of propaganda informs us about the term's
    true meaning and also clears up misunderstandings about the
    extent to which average Americans are subjected to
    propaganda. The broader purpose of providing us with this
    definition is to persuade us that advertising is indeed
    about the various techniques of propaganda so we can protect
    ourselves from its daily onslaughts.

2. "Seduced" and "brainwashed" are both words with strong
    negative connotations; we are likely to be shocked or
    disbelieving when we read that "Americans, adults and
    children alike, are being seduced. They are being
    brainwashed" (1). By using these terms, McClintock
    challenges our belief in our independence and free will.
    Through the use of these and other terms ("victims"), she
    provokes us to continue reading the essay. Ironically, this
    use of loaded words manipulates the readers' reactions in a
    manner similar to that of propaganda.

3. Questions appear in the discussions of Glittering
    Generalities and Card Stacking and in the conclusion to the
    essay. In both the sections on propaganda techniques, the
    questions are rhetorical, in that they need no answers. They
    are questions used to make a point. For example, McClintock
    asks, "After all, how can anyone oppose 'truth, justice, and
    the American way'?" (6). The implied answer is, "No one
    can." In her discussion of specific empty phrases, the
    author asks questions to point out the meaninglessness of
    such statements as "He cares..." and "Vote for Progress" (7).
    These questions are meant not to be answered, but to show the
    vagueness of glittering generalities. In the section on
    card-stacking (18-20), she suggests that readers ask
    questions to test the validity of a political accusation such
    as "my opponent has changed his mind five times...." The
    questions in the essay's conclusion, however, are real
    questions to which she provides answers.

4. Tied to McClintock's explanation of why propaganda works
    is a warning: that to remain blind to the power of propaganda
    is to consent "to handing over our independence, our
    decision-making ability, and our brains to the advertisers"
    (24). In order to prevent this fate, McClintock advises us
    to do the work that clear thinking requires. This ending is
    an example of a call-for-action conclusion.

INDIVIDUAL AND GROUP IDENTITY

Desmond Morris

Questions for Close Reading (p. 541)

1. The thesis appears in paragraph 3: "Property, as owned
    space which is displayed as owned space, is a special
    kind of sharing system which reduces fighting much more than
    it causes it."

2. Territories tend to restrict the natural tendency of
    humans to compete for domination because they give us each
    private space in which we are dominant (3). Since the
    possession of property makes individuals likely to fight to
    protect their space from invasion, potential invaders are
    usually dissuaded. Humans mark off their territories in
    primarily visual ways.

3. People hunger for a sense of belonging and identity that
    the vastness of a nation cannot satisfy (7). As a result,
    they form "subgroups" within a nation--small, local,
    fraternal or professional associations in which individuals
    are more visible. Groups such as clubs, gangs, unions, and
    political parties are examples of such subgroups that supply
    the feeling of belonging to a small tribe.

4. When our personal space is unavoidably entered, we allow
    it to shrink. If our personal space is severely limited, as
    in a crowded elevator, we are likely to adopt avoidance
    techniques (15). For example, we may ignore the presence of
    others, converting them into "nonpersons"--trying not to face
    them, make eye contact, or touch them more than necessary.

5. conglomeration (7): mixture of miscellaneous things
    portals (8): doorways
    demarcation (11): boundary, limit
    alienation (19): the state of being withdrawn or detached
    proximity (20): closeness

Questions About the Writer's Craft (p. 542)

1. Morris names three types of territory: tribal, family,
    and personal. These types are classified according to the
    size of the group. Tribal territories are subdivided into
    nations and subgroups within nations such as societies,
    clubs, and political parties. Family territories are
    classifed into the territory of the home, with its two parts,
    the public and private, and the "staked-out"
    home-away-from-home. Personal space is subdivided into our
    own "portable territory"--"elbow room" (16) and shared space
    or "cocooning" (20).

2. Not until paragraph 6 does Morris begin to analyze his
    first classification, tribal territory. He spends the first
    five paragraphs defining the concept of territory and
    explaining its purpose in human society.

3. Morris uses enumeration transitions set off as short
    headings to introduce his major divisions (paragraphs 6, 11,
    and 15). Within the sections and within paragraphs, Morris
    uses a variety of short transitional phrases; many refer to
    time or are indicative of a mood or opinion; see paragraphs 7
    ("Today"), 11 ("Often"), and 12 ("Only when") for transitions
    of time, and paragraphs 9 ("Indeed"), 12 ("Unfortunately"),
    17 ("Of course"), 18 ("Unfortunately"), and 20 ("Of course")
    for examples of transitions expressing a tone or opinion.

Morris also uses many sentence openers such as "If" (18), "But" (14), "As" (11), and "However" (17) to indicate the start of a new idea. Throughout the essay as a whole, transitions are clearly marked.

4. This article appears to be directed at the reader who is educated and interested in the world of ideas, but who is not a specialist in sociology or anthropology. Morris uses an easy-to-read style, with a very comprehensible vocabulary and fairly short sentences; his paragraphs are medium in length, but since he makes extensive use of examples as his means of development, the paragraphs are very accessible. As support, Morris offers only explanation and examples, rather than the hard facts that a specialist in the field would demand.

ARGUMENTATION-PERSUASION

OPENING COMMENTS

        Freshman composition courses often end with
argumentation-persuasion. There are good reasons for this.
Since an argumentation-persuasion essay can be developed using a
number of rhetorical patterns, it makes sense to introduce this
mode after students have had experience using a variety of
patterns. Then, too, argumentation-persuasion demands logical
reasoning and sensitivity to the nuances of language. We've
found that earlier papers--causal analysis and descriptive
writing, for example--help students develop the reasoning and
linguistic skills needed to tackle this final assignment.
        When teaching argumentation-persuasion, we stress that
the pattern makes special demands. Not only do writers have to
generate convincing support for their positions, but they also
must acknowledge and deal with opposing points of view. Having
to contend with a contrary viewpoint challenges students to dig
into their subjects so they can defend their position with
conviction. Students should find the material on pages 557-59
helpful, for it illustrates different ways to acknowledge and
deal with the opposition.
        Despite their initial moans and groans of protest,
students enjoy the challenge of argumentation-persuasion. To
help them become more aware of the characteristics of this
rhetorical pattern, we often ask them to look through current
newspapers and magazines and clip editorials and advertisements
they find effective. In class, these items provide the basis for
a lively discussion about the strategies unique to
argumentation-persuasion. For example, the endorsement of a
health club by a curvaceous television celebrity raises the issue
of credibility or ethos. An editorial filled with highly
charged language ("We must unite to prevent this boa constrictor
of a highway from strangling our neighborhood") focuses
attention on the connotative power of words.
        Both of us often conclude our composition courses with
an assignment based on a controversial issue. Depending on the
time available and the skill of our students, the assignment may
or may not require outside research. If it does call for
research, we begin by having the class as a whole brainstorm as
many controversial social issues as they can. Then, for each
issue, the class generates a pair of propositions representing
opposing viewpoints. We've listed below a few examples of what
our classes typically come up with:

Controversial Subject	Propositions
School prayer	Prayer in public schools should be allowed or prayer in public schools should not be allowed.
Drug abuse in professional sports	Professional sports should implement a mandatory program of drug testing or professional sports should not implement a mandatory program of drug testing.

| Adoption | Adopted children should be given the means to contact their biological parents or adopted children should not be given the means to contact their biological parents. |

If the assignment does not include research, we focus attention on more immediate local problems. Using the sequence described above, we start the activity by asking the class as a whole to brainstorm as many controversial campus problems as they can. We've listed below several examples of this activity:

Controversial Subject	Propositions
Cheating	A student found guilty of cheating on an exam or paper should be suspended or a student found guilty of cheating on an exam or paper should not be suspended.
Fraternities and sororities	Fraternities and sororities should be banned from campus or fraternities and sororities should not be banned from campus.
Drinking	The college pub should be licensed to serve liquor or the college pub should not be licensed to serve liquor.

Once the propositions have been generated, the activity can go in one of two directions. We might ask students to pair up by issue, with the students in each pair taking opposing positions. Or we might have students select a position on any issue identified by the class, without being concerned that both sides of an issue are covered. In any case, students base their argumentation-persuasion essays on the proposition they selected. Though they may eventually qualify their propositions, starting with a definitive thesis helps focus students' work in the early stages of the activity.

We try to schedule the assignment so there is enough time at the end of the course for students to deliver their arguments orally. The presentations take about one class, and we call this class either "Forum on Contemporary Social Issues" or "Forum on Critical Campus Issues." Students tell us that they enjoy and learn a good deal from these brief oral presentations. (We do not, by the way, grade the talks--just the papers.)

Both of us have been pleased by the way this final activity energizes students, pulling them out of the inevitable end-of-semester slump during which daydreams of holiday parties or reunions with high school friends may take precedence over academic matters. The forum does indeed create a kind of learning fellowship--certainly not a bad way to end the course.

This chapter's professional readings illustrate the mix of logical support and emotional appeal characteristic of argumentation-persuasion. To develop her proposition that children's violent play does not necessarily lead to aggressive acts, Marzollo relates her experiences as a mother and thus establishes her ethos on the subject. Similarly, Krents, blind from birth, draws upon his own life to develop his thesis that society is insensitive to the disabled. Rosenblatt narrates

99

a dramatic and poignant story to support his proposition about
human behavior, while Twain uses a stream of scathing examples to
dramatize his sharply contrasting view of "The Damned Human
Race." Although not as cynical as Twain, Tutko and Bruns, as
well as Trippett, also build their arguments around a series of
compelling examples. Finally, several essays are particularly
helpful for illustrating different ways of dealing with opposing
arguments. In two otherwise quite different selections, both
Fussell's "The Boy Scout Handbook" and Meade's "One Vote for This
Age of Anxiety" begin by mentioning the opposition before going
on to assert a contrary point of view. And to discredit his
opponents, Wainwright deliberately uses charged emotional
language, hoping that his no-holds-barred approach will win
readers to his side.

MY PISTOL-PACKING KIDS

Jean Marzollo

Questions for Close Reading (p. 581)

1. Marzollo reveals her main idea about children's war play
   very gradually, so that we begin to know her position only
   starting with paragraph 13. Essentially, she implies her
   thesis. One way of expressing it might be: "Children's
   violent play is useful and necessary to their emotional
   growth."

2. Children "play at violence," Marzollo says, because they
   want to learn about all sides of life, not just the pleasant
   "mittens and kittens side." Playing with toy weapons and
   pretending to commit violent acts helps them to deal with the
   "underside of their lives," the side that is full of
   imaginary frightening creatures that threaten to do them harm
   (13). In other words, mastering "gun play" gives them a
   sense they can beat back what scares them, in their dreams or
   in real life. In paragraph 23, Marzollo elaborates what she
   means. "Fantasy play...allows children to blow off a lot of
   steam." Through these fantasies children can feel some sense
   of power, when actually they are totally under the domination
   of parents, teachers, and other adults. "On some level," the
   author writes, "every child lives with tyrants" (23).

3. Watching her own kids grow, Marzollo has realized that
   "at the ripe old ages of five and seven...they are at the
   ages when they know what they see on TV is not real."
   However, younger children of three or four, she implies, do
   worry that TV characters and monsters might attack them (6).
   Later in the essay, Marzollo imagines her two sons growing
   out of the need for violent play; she anticipates a later
   stage of childhood when "on their own ... they will realize
   eventually that fantasy violence is for little kids" (30).
   At that older age, they will move on to real activities that
   let them experience a sense of mastery and power, such as
   sports, science projects, music lessons, and so on. Marzollo
   views children as preoccupied with fantasy during a middle
   stage of childhood, between perhaps five and seven years of
   age.

4. Fantasy play with toy guns is "refined," according to the author, because it calls into action all the children's abilities to organize a scenario and play it out. Marzollo even provides a sample "script" of such a play conversation between her sons (18-22), showing how they act like little film directors setting up scenes and then performing them. She calls such play "effective" because it is a kind of "therapy," helping kids to "release frustrations and experience illusory control" (24-25). Finally, such play is "safe" because the guns are only toys, and no one gets hurt for real. Children, she maintains, "don't want to get hurt and they know how not to" (26). Even psychologically, the games are safe. The children switch around the roles of victim and aggressor: "Every child I have watched can play both roles" (25), and there really are no victors. "The game is safe emotionally as well as physically" (28).

5. stalwart (7): morally strong
   legitimacy (8): correctness, validity
   condoning (14): overlook, make excuses for
   improvise (18): invent or perform without preparation
   vengeance (27): with great violence or fury

Questions About the Writer's Craft   (p. 582)

1. Marzollo's expertise on this subject clearly comes from her attentive and thoughtful experience as a parent, and so she chooses first person as the most natural and effective way of presenting her observations about children's gun play. Her approach is not theoretical, but practical, which would appeal to many general readers. She comes across as an earnest, concerned and even original thinker on this subject, and as such she is very persuasive.

2. The introduction first shows the mother's perception of her children as "sweet and quiet" as they draw at the kitchen table, and then dramatically reveals the subject of her children's drawings: "lurid outer space battles" (1). This contrast between her view of the children as innocent and the reality that they love violence establishes her main theme. Why are such sweet children addicted to violent play? Marzollo goes on to explain that in fact such play at wars and battles serves a purpose in children's emotional development. She comes to the conclusion that children embody both sides of the contrast: even while they adore violent games, they are still innocent.

3. By using direct quotations, Marzollo can let us experience more directly how she handles toy guns in the home and how the children's make-believe violence involves some high-level skills. In paragraph 15, Marzollo shows us her reaction when a child points a gun at her: "Don't point that rifle at me because it reminds me of a real gun and I don't like real guns." Through these words, she directly demonstrates that she, as an adult, rejects gun play for herself, while permitting it for her children. In paragraphs 19-22, she lets us overhear the children at play, being alternately "directors" and participants, giving instructions one second and exuberantly playing out a violent scene the next. The quotations serve as evidence that her decision to condone play battles is a valid one.

4. Rhetorical questions appear in paragraphs 2, 9, 28, and 30, and are most often used to help Marzollo move her argument along. In paragraph 2, she asks, "...what made them grow up and want to create things like this? Repeatedly?" This cry focuses our attention on her bafflement about children's love of violence and her search for the reasons

for it. In paragraph 9, she proposes a hypothetical global
boycott of violent media and toys and questions how far such
a ban would extend. "But what about the sticks, yarn, and
crayons? Should we take them, too?" This question shows
Marzollo recognizing the objections to the censoring of war
toys: such toys are hard to define, for children can turn
anything into a toy weapon. In paragraph 28, in a question
directly addressed to the reader, she forces us to take into
account the paradoxical safety of "gun play": "Have you ever
noticed that in mock violent play no one ever wins or loses?"
Finally, as she makes her last point, that fantasy violence
is a necessary stage of childhood, she asks, "What's for big
kids? Real violence?" This rhetorical question anticipates
a last objection we might have to her permissiveness about
toy guns; her response, "No...," moves our attention to her
next point: that children grow into another stage in which
they learn sophisticated, reality-based ways of feeling
strong and in control.

THE BOY SCOUT HANDBOOK

Paul Fussell

Questions for Close Reading (p. 589)

1. Fussell's thesis is implied. One way of stating it might
    be: "The Official Boy Scout Handbook is full of
    practical advice and ethical guidance that everyone in our
    society should take seriously."

2. The revised Boy Scout Handbook shows changes that
    bring it up to date with modern times. For example, the
    uniform is more contemporary, with trousers, not "breeches,"
    and with a variety of modern hats, including a visor. An
    awareness of recent national and international history
    results in such changes as a new left-handed handshake that
    will not offend the third world as the old one would (5).
    When groups of scouts are pictured, black faces are always
    included. And to the list of Great Americans have been added
    such labor and civil rights figures as Walter Reuther, Samuel
    Gompers, Harriet Tubman, Martin Luther King, and Whitney
    Young. Also, a post-Watergate consciousness has led the
    writers to caution scouts to stay informed and change what is
    not good (6). Other contemporary touches include the
    downplaying of knots, the renaming of artificial respiration
    as rescue breathing, and the inclusion of the metric system.
    The main change, however, is one of tone, according to
    Fussell; "throughout there is a striking new lyricism," he
    writes, and "more emphasis now on fun and less on duty" (6).

3. Some of the Handbook's "good sense" is practical:
    advice on starting and putting out fires and swimming safely
    (7, 8), for example. But much of the sensible advice
    concerns ethics and psychology. "The constant moral theme,"
    writes Fussell, "is the inestimable benefits of looking
    objectively outward and losing consciousness of self in the
    work to be done." In light of this point, the book cautions
    against "anxious self-absorption" and "trips" and trances"
    (7). "But the best advice is ethical," the author believes,
    and gives as examples such maxims as "'Learn to think,'
    'Gather knowledge,' 'Have initiative,' 'Respect the rights of
    others'" (8).

4. Fussell finds the book errs in two ways--it reiterates
   the term "free world" too often, presumably to stress
   anti-communism, and it is "insistent" in its "Deism." As an
   example, he cites the instructions for being lost in the
   woods; in addition to staying put, the scout is told to "have
   faith that someone will find you" and that "prayer will
   help." He likewise objects to the definition of the United
   States as a country "whose people believe in a supreme
   being." These flaws are not very serious in Fussell's eyes.
   The religiosity is balanced by extreme fairness, in which
   every reference to "your church" is followed by "or
   synagogue"; overall, Fussell concludes, the Handbook's
   "religiosity is so broad it's harmless" (6).

5. humanistic (1): concerning humans and their values,
                   abilities and achievements
   incipient (2): in the initial stages, commencing
   fascism (2): political movement characterized by
               dictatorship, governmental control of private
               enterprise, belligerent nationalism and militarism
   ascription (3): attribution
   empiric (5): one who believes that practical experience
               is the sole source of knowledge
   unambiguously (6): clearly
   compendia (7): summaries containing essential information
               in brief form

Questions About the Writer's Craft (p. 589)

   1. Fussell weaves opposing viewpoints throughout the
   article, especially in the introduction, conclusion, and
   paragraph 6. In the introduction (1-2), Fussell discusses at
   some length the "liberal intellectuals," who "have often
   gazed uneasily at the Boy Scout movement" because it has
   military and chauvinistic origins and trappings. He reports
   that the deism, flag worshipping, and third-rate artistry of
   Norman Rockwell also have offended "those of exquisite
   taste." These criticisms ultimately serve as a platform for
   his praise for the movement's revised guidebook: "But anyone
   who imagines that the scouting movement is either sinister or
   stupid or funny should spend a few hours with the latest
   edition of The Official Boy Scout Handbook" (3). In the
   conclusion (9), Fussell criticizes George Orwell for his
   cynical rejection of wholesome children's literature, using
   this as a jumping off place for another strong recommendation
   of the Handbook.
        Right from the start, Fussell turns his discussion
   of the Boy Scout movement's critics to his own advantage
   by using loaded terms for his opponents ("the right
   sort of people," "liberal intellectuals," "those of exquisite
   taste," "the enlightened"); some readers may become biased
   against these critics because of these terms. Fussell's
   original audience for the review, however, probably included
   some of these "liberal intellectuals," who would find his
   critique of their biases intriguing. Fussell adds to his
   credibility with this group by being familiar with some of
   their favorite writers, Lionell Trilling and Kenneth Burke
   (1), and by quoting George Orwell (1, 9). To debunk the
   intellectuals' stereotype of the scoutmaster, he dryly
   equates Orwell's maxim, "All scoutmasters are
   homosexuals" with another extreme and foolish Orwellian
   remark, that 'All tobacconists are Fascists."
        Fussell also counters possible objections in paragraph 6,
   where he discusses two problems he himself has with the
   handbook: its blatant anti-communism and its deism. He pokes
   a bit of fun at the recommendation to pray when lost in the
   woods and then asserts that the religiosity is "so broad that
   it's harmless." (See answer #4 above.)

103

Another place where Fussell undoubtedly gets the "liberal intellectuals" on his side is paragraph 8, where he applies the ethics of the Handbook to the "gross official misbehavior of the seventies," wryly producing such propostions as "A scout does not tap his acquaintances' telephone," and "A scout does not bomb and invade a neutral country, and then lie about it."

2. While Fussell comments that "a complex sentence is as rare as a reference to girls" (3) in the Boy Scout Handbook, long and complex sentences are certainly not rare in his essay. On the basis of such stylistic features as a sophisticated vocabulary, complex sentences, and heightened style ("It betokens no access"; "it happily embraces the one to avoid any truck with the other" (4)), we can assume Fussell intended this review for a sophisticated audience, probably college- rather than high-school educated. Since the content is essentially a defense of the Handbook, these educated readers are probably opponents of the Boy Scout tradition, perhaps even those "liberal intellectuals" mentioned in paragraph 2.

3. Fussell's comparisons often startle in their originality and usually treat the subject at hand with light humor. For example, he compares the Boy Scout Handbook to The Red Cross First Aid Manual, The World Almanac, and the Gideon Bible, in being one of the country's most well-known books; he also compares the supposed founder, William Hillcourt, to such other fake culture "heroes" as Ann Page and Reddy Kilowatt (3). He defines the style of the Handbook by using a unique comparison: "a complex sentence is as rare as a reference to girls" (3). In paragraph 4, he compares Boy Scouting to the Roman Catholic Church in having a pragmatic strategy for coping with change, and in paragraph 5, he dryly likens the new variety of scout caps to those worn by General Westmoreland and sunbelt retirees.

4. The Boy Scout Handbook is not perfect, and Fussell increases his credibility with his readers by allowing for its flaws. He finds these defects harmless, however, and tends to treat them lightly by simply pointing them out with only a brief ironic comment. He lists many of the movement's superficial weak points in paragraphs 2, 3, and 4, and uses wit to put them in perspective (see answer # 3 above). In paragraphs 5 and 7, he makes light of the Handbook's preoccupation with trivial details: "shorts are still in," and "a paste of meat tenderizer is the best remedy for insect stings." In 6, he satirizes the impractical religiosity of the recommendations to carry the Bible along on camping trips and to pray when lost in the forest.

DARKNESS AT NOON

Harold Krents

Questions for Close Reading (p. 594)

1. Krents' thesis is implied. One way of stating it could
   be: "People often treat the handicapped as if they were
   totally incompetent, but a more acceptable reaction would be
   to presume competence."

2. People sometimes react to him as if he is unable to hear
   as well as unable to see. So, they shout, or, conversely,
   whisper about him in his presence as if he can't hear a
   slightly lowered voice. Also, some people act as if he can't
   talk, and so ask other people to tell them about him in his
   presence (4-14). The most significant misconception,
   however, is that his blindness keeps him from being able to
   work at his profession (15-16).

3. Readers can infer from the child's comment that the child
   cannot discern any difference in the performance of Krents
   and his father as they practice shooting baskets. The
   difference between a handicapped and a nonhandicapped person,
   in other words, is not always immediately apparent.
   Nonhandicapped people sometimes fail to perform tasks well,
   too.

4. Krents does not discuss any limitations, and he does
   seem, indeed, to have few, other than the obvious ones--he
   can't read a regular book or see faces and objects around
   him. On the other hand, the article does indicate he has a
   full range of activities, most of which he can do alone--he
   attended college and law school, passed the bar, traveled and
   studied in Europe, married, and even participated in a
   modified version of sports.

5. narcissistic (1): self-adoring, self-loving
   conversely (2): on the other hand, in contrast
   cum laude (15): "with honor" (used on diplomas)
   mandate (17): order, command, dictate

Questions About the Writer's Craft (p. 594)

1. The article uses climactic organization. It progresses
   from people's minor misconceptions about the blind to a
   misconception of major importance: that he could not work as
   a lawyer because of his blindness. At the conclusion of the
   article, Krents returns to the first misconception, that he
   can't hear, while using an anecdote that underscores his main
   point about the ability of handicapped persons to work. 2.
   When describing the minor ways people have misunderstood the
   nature and extent of his handicap, Krents' tone is light. He
   sums up each example with an ironic comment. Describing
   how ticket agents at airports will refer to him as a "76," he
   says, "Either they fear that if the dread word is spoken, the
   ticket agent's retina will immediately detach, or they are
   reluctant to inform me of my condition of which I may not
   have been previously aware" (3). His second example lets us
   know that sometimes he responds sarcastically when people
   treat him in an inappropriate manner; when waiters ask his
   wife if he would like a drink, he replies, "Indeed, he would"
   (4). He also describes a three-way conversation in which an
   admitting nurse and an orderly persisted despite his protests
   in acting as if he couldn't speak English. Krents does not,
   however, speak lightly when discussing the difficulties a
   blind person has finding employment. The humorous touches
   encourage us to like Krents, because he seems to have an

upbeat attitude about life and to be adjusted to his handicap. If he had related these experiences with bitterness, blame or self-pity, we would probably not be so inclined to accept him as a completely competent person. He keeps things in perspective, and this outlook gives him credibility.

3. The short paragraphs are very concise and make their points quickly; as a result, the essay is fast-paced and easy to read. Most students will probably appreciate Krents' willingness to touch lightly on the difficulties of being handicapped and will most likely agree that Krents is a sympathetic and convincing writer.

4. In making an argument for the fair and equal treatment of the handicapped in the area of employment, Krents does not provide much supporting evidence at all. While in other sections of the essay he offers experiences from his own life, in the discussion of employment he tells us only the general fact that he was turned down by over forty law firms. In paragraph 17, he only briefly mentions what changes are starting to occur. The article's purpose, however, is to use Krents' experiences to make a case for treating the handicapped as competent people, not to advocate hiring the handicapped. Given Krent's purpose and audience, his level of development works very well; had he developed this point in greater detail, he would have digressed from his main point.

A LITTLE BANNING IS A DANGEROUS THING

Loudon Wainwright

Questions for Close Reading (p. 600)

1. Wainwright's thesis is implied. One way of stating it might be, "Children need to read all sorts of books, without restriction, to grow and learn about themselves and the complexities of our world." Another possibility is: "Book banning does not serve children's best interests, because the books that are banned are often the best for kids to read."

2. Anthony Adverse's "good fortune" (3) at having a sexual encounter exhilarated the young Wainwright. He clearly felt delight--and sexual arousal--when he read the love scene. The "useful, educational purpose" it served is not specified, but students can guess that reading this novel informed the youthful Wainwright about sex and passion, parts of adult life normally hidden from children.

3. The book banners include a wide range of "alert vigilantes of the printed word," according to Wainwright. He mentions "outraged individual parents," teachers, ministers, and "such well organized watchdog outfits as the Gabler family of Texas, Washington's Heritage Foundation, and of course, the Moral Majority" (4). Their goal is to "keep the minds of children clean," Wainwright says (4), and he points out that it is very presumptuous of the censors to imagine they know what goes on in young minds (6).

4. Books fill many crucial childhood needs, Wainwright says. They afford a private world, a place away from adult demands (7). Also, books give children information that adults often try to shield them from--the knowledge that people do harm, for example (8). Reading can confirm for children that other people, like themselves, do not do right all the time, and that fantasies of revenge, conquest, and "outlandish wooings" are normal. Finally, books let children know that "life is rich and complicated and difficult"; they "offer opportunites, choices, and plausible models" (10). They are, ultimately, sources of truth.

5. lubricious (3): sexually stimulating
   ecstacy (3): bliss, intense joy
   depravity (3): moral corruption
   vigilantes (4): people organized to suppress and punish
                   crime outside the system of law
   potboiler (11): a sensational work, usually of poor
                   quality, written for quick profit

Questions About the Writer's Craft (p. 601)

1. Wainwright sarcastically calls would-be censors "righteous book banners" (3) and "assorted crusaders." Other vivid phrases with negative overtones include "the cleansing fire" (4); "wretched little war to keep the minds of children clean" (4); "weird presumption" (6); "the bleak, cramped, sanitized, fear-ridden state of many adults..." (9). These negative descriptions verge on mockery, indicating the strength of Wainwright's opposition to censorship and his conviction that book-banners are ignorant. Readers may be prejudiced against the censors on the basis of these terms.

2. Wainwright cleverly plays on the familiar quotation, "A little learning is a dangerous thing" (from "An Essay on Criticism" by Alexander Pope). Not only does the word "banning" fit in well rhythmically and grammatically, but, since Wainwright's thesis is that banning inhibits learning, the twist is very effective: it startles and attracts the reader's attention, and it states the theme in a catchy way. Wainwright shows that banning is dangerous because it limits children's access to a full range of reading experiences.

3. The farming image of the first sentence conveys the receptivity of the young mind. In this case, Wainwright's mind was "planted" with sexual awareness gained from Anthony Adverse. In addition to representing the author's state of mind when he read the sexy chapter, however, the image of planting a seed plays upon the subject of the essay--sexy reading as permissable, even beneficial, for adolescents, and necessary to their growth.

4. The tone of the conclusion is rather lighthearted and a touch nostalgic. Referring to a sexy book he read late in life, Lady Chatterley's Lover, the author asserts that such books are appreciated more in youth than in old age. This works well as a conclusion in that it drives his main point home with a strong personal statement.

THE MAN IN THE WATER

Roger Rosenblatt

<u>Questions</u> <u>for</u> <u>Close</u> <u>Reading</u> (p. 606)

1. The thesis can be found at the end of paragraph 2: "Last Wednesday, the elements, indifferent as ever, brought down Flight 90. And on that same afternoon, human nature--groping and flailing in mysteries of its own--rose to the occasion."

2. Most people in the plane were saved successfully. In addition, the crash gave people a chance to demonstrate that humans could successfully combat the disaster caused by nature. The people who helped in the rescue showed great courage and humanity. The helicopter team risked a crash whenever they descended to the water to pull out victims; the passerby who dived in to help a woman reach shore acted against his own best interest in order to save the life of another. And finally, the unknown victim who passed the flotation ring to the other victims rather than be pulled to safety himself showed a heroic yet tragic commitment to human life--tragic, because he drowned before he could be rescued.

3. The crash occurred in downtown Washington, D.C., a place normally bustling with the orderly functions of our national government. The plane hit a bridge, and so it was a double disaster, disrupting traffic in the air and on the ground. Also, the tropical motif of Air Florida contrasted sharply with the wintry landscape. Finally, the urban location made it easy for the media to follow the rescue closely and for television cameras to capture the drama.

4. The man won his fight to save the lives of others. In this success, he demonstrated the greatest heroism possible to humanity--the ability to fight against the destructive forces of nature and to help others live.

5. <u>emblemized</u> (1): symbolized
   <u>aesthetic</u> (1): pertaining to artwork or taste in beauty
   <u>implacable</u> (9): relentless, merciless

<u>Questions</u> <u>About</u> <u>the</u> <u>Writer's</u> <u>Craft</u> (606)

1. At the end of paragraph 4, the essay shifts away from describing the events of the crash and rescue. In the paragraphs following, Rosenblatt moves to interpreting the man's selfless behavior for the reader, giving his actions a particular coloring in order to achieve a purpose--to persuade us the man was not only a hero, but the best humanity has to offer. Specifically, paragraphs 5 and 6 appeal to our emotions by presenting the hypothetical thoughts of the unknown hero before, during and after the crash. Paragraph 7 also uses pathos in comparing the caring man to uncaring nature and suggesting that the human was in fierce combat with unfeeling nature. Rosenblatt thus leads us to identify with the hero and feel he was a common man of uncommon spirit.

2. Rosenblatt underplays the crash because he is setting the stage for the drama of the rescue. He portrays the disaster as common, almost routine, in a world where crashes and accidents are frequent. Against this background, human efforts to set all to rights seem all the more noteworthy and commendable.

3. Starting with paragraph 5, we learn the unknown man's possible thoughts as he rides the plane, as the fatal descent begins, and as he struggles in the water to help others. This switch to his subjective state of mind may lead us to sympathize with him, to care about him as a special individual, and to appreciate that he was like us. By the time he sinks beneath the waters of the Potomac, we may feel a sense of loss ourselves.

4. The essay begins by invoking the contrasts between the orderly governmental city and the sudden disruption of the wreck; between the winter setting and the tropically decorated vacation plane; between the normally heavy air traffic over the city and the single fallen plane. Paragraph 2 introduces the contrasts between the failure of the machine and the idea of a human success, and between the elements and human nature, two contrasts that recur in the essay in paragraphs 7 and 9. Then, in paragraph 3, we meet the three identifiable heroes who survived, and who contrast with the unknown hero who died. The oppositions between nature, "making no distinctions of good and evil, acting on no principles, offering no lifelines," and the man, "acting wholly on distinctions, principles, and, one supposes, on faith" (7), help us appreciate the essence of what it means to be human, as distinct from just a creature of nature.

THE DAMNED HUMAN RACE

Mark Twain

Questions for Close Reading (615)

1. Twain states his thesis in the first paragraph: "For it obliges me to renounce my allegiance to the Darwinian theory of the Ascent of Man from the Lower Animals; since it now seems plain to me that that theory ought to be vacated in favor of a new and truer one, this new and truer one to be named the Descent of Man from the Higher Animals." By this, Twain is humorously suggesting that humans beings' "traits and dispositions" are lower, not higher, than those of the other creatures.

2. Twain discovers humans have a long list of negative characteristics. He finds them cruel (4, 10), avaricious and miserly (5), vengeful (7), morally loose (7, 8), and indecent and vulgar (9). Humans are also the only animals to wage war (11), invade other countries (12), take slaves (13), and show patriotism (14). They are, somewhat paradoxically, both religious--hence intolerant of others with different beliefs (15)-- and reasoning--though Twain prefers to think of them as maniacs (16). Overall, Twain finds the defect that will forever prevent humans from ever beginning "to approach even the meanest of the Higher Animals" is what he terms the "moral sense" (19-20), "the ability to distinguish good from evil; and with it, necessarily, the ability to do evil" (21).

3. The earl and his party of sportsmen killed seventy-two buffalo, feasted on one, and left the seventy-one others to rot. The anaconda, in a scientific test conducted by Twain, killed only what he wanted to eat, and no more, although Twain provided him with seven calves in all. This "experiment" shows that the snake is less cruel and less wasteful than an earl, and therefore a superior creature.

4. Humans have "occasion to blush" because they feel shame about their bodies, and, having a "soiled mind," feel natural behavior to be indecent. Twain points out that people cover themselves, even their chests and backs, because they are horrified at the possibility of "indecent suggestion" (9). Also, humans consciously practice cruel and loose sexual behavior such as keeping harems, behavior about which they should blush. When animals are loose in their morals, Twain says, it is because they are totally innocent.

5. confounded (3): confused
   anaconda (4): a type of large snake
   wantonly (4): excessively, wastefully
   chicane (5): trickery, deceit
   heretics (10): people who openly disagree with the church
   constitutionally (19): by nature, inherently
   ineradicable (19): not removable, unerasable
   smirchless (22): without a stain, without dishonor

Questions About the Writer's Craft (p. 615)

1. Twain humorously claims to have used the scientific method in order to put his credibility on a par with that of scientists. He pretends to have conducted experiments, and by this device he satirizes not only human evil and cruelty but also the arrogance of our presuming to be superior to all other creatures and exercising this "superiority" by turning the other creatures into laboratory specimens. Ultimately, Twain shows that the standard the scientists, and people in general, use to decide what constitutes a "higher" species is invalid. Using a moral yardstick, rather than an evolutionary one, Twain demonstrates that humans are really the lowest of the creatures.

2. Many of Twain's examples of human inferiority are shocking, starting with his example of the hunting earl. In paragraph 10, Twain provides a list of atrocious cruelties from human history that most students will certainly find shocking; he mentions mutilations, gougings, flaying, imprisonment, and burning as punishment for small offenses or religious disagreements, and, conversely, minor punishments, such as a ten-shilling fine, for incredible cruelties. Also, in paragraph 15, Twain uses very strong language to discuss human religious intolerance; some students will be shocked because they are used to hearing religions spoken of deferentially. For example, Twain writes that man "cuts his neighbor's throat if his theology isn't straight," and "has made a graveyard of the globe" in trying to spread his religions. Such shocking examples and language help Twain to convince us that his main point is valid--humans are cruel and inferior creatures.

3. One or two examples would be sufficient to support his idea that humans are inferior to other creatures, but Twain piles on examples to dramatize his point. He wants to show that such atrocities are not isolated and rare, but habitual and common among the human species. For example, he shows us in paragraph 10 that every era of history and every people of the world have engaged in vicious punishments and inhumane justice.

4. Absurdity appears in this essay in the form of Twain's "experiments," ridiculous studies confronting humans and animals with moral choices. It is certainly unlikely that he tested an anaconda's killer instinct with seven calves (4) or "furnished a hundred different kinds of wild and tame animals the opportunity to accumulate vast stores of food"

(5). And his claim to have put a mixture of human races and
religions in a cage to see if they could learn to get along
is also far-fetched (18). Ironically, the morbid details of
Twain's essay come from human history: they are not creations
of the writer's mind, but examples of actual human violence
(4, 10, 11). As Twain notes in paragraph 16, the human
record "is the fantastic record of a maniac." So, the essay
does contain elements of black humor, and its conclusion,
"And so I find we have descended and degenerated, from some
far ancestor....Below us--nothing," is dark indeed.

TO WIN OR NOT TO WIN: THAT IS THE QUESTION

James Bruns and William Tutko

Questions for Close Reading (p. 625)

1. The authors present their thesis in paragraph 3:
    "Winning...is an insatiable greed" (3); its satisfactions are
    undermined or negated by the obsessive need to achieve even
    higher goals, better stats, or more wins.

2. Tutko and Bruns provide a wide range of winners, selected
    from some of the most popular and prominent competitive
    activities in American life. Collegiate and professional
    team sports are represented in their discussion of football
    and basketball coaches and players. Individual sports stars
    like Jimmy Connors and Chris Evert appear as winners caught
    in the endless cycle of proving themselves. Also, the
    authors discuss politicians as examples of nonsports
    competitors who are also consumed by the need to win again
    and again.

3. In paragraphs 9 and 10, the authors cite the roles of
    aggression, survival, and defiance in our earliest national
    origins and suggest that American history and culture make us
    inherently competitive. Not only does this preoccupation
    with victory go back to our beginnings, but, the authors
    feel, our country's present value system holds winning as one
    of the most important things in both personal life and
    national politics. Later in the essay, they expand this idea
    that Americans measure everything by how much progress has
    been made (19). Finally, they point to the Judeo-Christian
    ethic and its emphasis that hard work is a virtue to be
    rewarded by success (20).

4. Victorious athletes must prove over and over to scores of
    challengers that they are worthy of their status by winning
    again. Often, they feel compelled to train ever more
    arduously to stay in top condition. They lose their privacy,
    for the press, the public, and the promoters beleaguer them
    with questions, personal criticisms, and business deals.
    Should athletes or teams lose, however, they become classifed
    immediately by the fickle fans as "bums"; paradoxically, if
    they win too much or too easily, they are accused of "ruining
    the game." As a result, sports championship can be "a hollow
    trip" and a very lonely experience. The authors clearly
    doubt that such championship is worth the high price.

5. insatiable (3): incapable of being satisfied
   permeates (10): penetrates, pervades
   emanating (10): flowing
   camaraderie (17): spirit of goodwill among friends or
                     colleagues
   clamoring (22): noisy, demanding

Questions About the Writer's Craft (p. 625)

1. The authors name some causes of our sports mania in
   paragraphs 9, 19, and 20, where they discuss our history and
   traditions, the general competitiveness of our culture, and
   our work ethic. They mention numerous effects of
   competitiveness. Right at the start, in the first paragraph,
   they point out the sports-engendered delusion that winning
   "proves" we're Number One." Another effect is the
   compulsion to win over and over, to keep proving ourselves.
   Finally, the authors list numerous consequences that fame and
   success exact from the public and private life of the typical
   driven athlete. In addition to developing the essay with
   cause and effect, the authors use numerous examples.

2. The many quotations reveal first-hand the mentality of
   victory-crazed Americans. The effect of presenting these
   examples bluntly, without transitions adds even more shock
   value to the aggressive and egotistical comments that
   comprise the "winning creed" of America's heroes. In
   parentheses, the authors critique this sports philosophy,
   sometimes sarcastically.

3. "Fundamental faith in the goodness of sports" (1),
   "competitive madness" (5), "competitive instinct" (10),
   "winning creed" (11), and "fanaticism" (25) are the other
   terms the authors use to characterize the American
   preoccupation with winning. These phrases are drawn from the
   languages of psychology and religion, and they convey
   connotations of mental illness and irrational religious
   faith. You may want to discuss how such highly connotative
   language can be a factor in unfairly slanting the argument
   against sports and competition.

4. Drinking salt water is unhealthy and even dangerous; at
   the very least, it will make you thirstier for fresh water.
   Likewise, winning can make you crave more victory. Using
   this striking comparison allows Tutko and Bruns to emphasize
   the danger they see in winning: it exacerbates the thirst for
   something to prop up our egos, to make us feel we are "Number
   one." Some students will recognize that the simile is
   ironic, because it undercuts our usual image of winning and
   success as positive achievements.

A RED LIGHT FOR SCOFFLAWS

Frank Trippett

<u>Questions</u> <u>for</u> <u>Close</u> <u>Reading</u> (p. 630)

1. Trippett states his main point in the second sentence: "Yet it is painfully apparent that millions of Americans who would never think of themselves as lawbreakers, let alone criminals, are taking increasing liberties with the legal codes that are designed to protect and nourish their society."

2. These days, routine violations of basic traffic laws constitute the most common and dangerous "scofflawry," according to Trippett (3). Such violations as running red lights and exceeding the speed limit are dangerous, of course, because people can and do get killed in car accidents; this danger is increased as Americans come to accept--and more widely practice-- these traffic violations as routine driving habits.

3. In paragraph 5, Trippett makes the point that most violators of laws and rules do so furtively; they pretend (hence hypocrisy) to be following the rules, that is, to be virtuous. Such furtiveness or hypocrisy is at least an honoring of the law, a superficial respect for it. Trippett fears we are losing even this surface homage to law-abidingness. Thus, "furtiveness," he says, "is the true outlaw's salute to the force of law-and-order."

4. Underneath the tendency to ignore the rules of the road lies a disrespect for law and order itself. Trippett fears this disrespect will unravel our society: "...society cannot help being harmed by any repetitious and brazen display of contempt for the fundamentals of order" (5). He cites as an example of the spread of lawlessness the fact that children entering school these days do not know the basic rules of being in a group. The problem goes beyond "etiquette," Trippett says, because drivers disregarding traffic laws have shown a tendency to take the law into their own hands and do violence to other cars and drivers (7).

5. <u>illicit</u> (1): illegal
<u>blithely</u> (1): casually, heedlessly
<u>derelictions</u> (1): delinquencies, acts of negligence
<u>flouting</u> (5): defying
<u>brazen</u> (5): brash, shamelss
<u>incivility</u> (7): rudeness
<u>nullify</u> (8): invalidate

<u>Questions</u> <u>About</u> <u>the</u> <u>Writer's</u> <u>Craft</u> (p. 630)

1. Trippett widens the scope of his essay very gradually; in paragraph 5 he begins to speak more abstractly about the "deep dents in the social mood" caused by scofflawry, and he ends with the assertion that "society cannot help being harmed" by the continued display of disrespect for the law. By paragraph 6, the reader becomes aware that his theme is broader than just traffic violators. He states that "the scofflaw spirit is pervasive" and mentions that schoolchildren today are ignorant of common rules of civilized behavior in a group.

   While his discussion of traffic violations is specific and filled with examples, Trippett doesn't provide much support for the idea that scofflawry is becoming rampant in all areas of society--and students may recognize the "slippery slope" fallacy here. In reality, the fact that people commonly violate certain sorts of rules is not a justification for asserting that rule violations will soon come to pervade society as a whole. Trippett's other argument is the analogy with the Prohibition era; this may seem convincing at first, but actually, while history can help guide policy decisions, there is no logical correlation between lawlessness during Prohibition and the spread of scofflawry today. Trippett's argument for the spreading of scofflawry is thus based on weak logic.

2. Statistics convincingly back up Trippett's point that drunk driving is lethal and that speeding is a highly practiced violation (3). Where he alleges that other kinds of social violations are increasing, he would be more credible if he used facts and figures. For example, to what extent are school children ignorant of how to get along together (6)? How common are tax cheating, littering, graffiti-writing, drug abuse, and so forth (2)? Trippett never provides hard evidence about these social problems.

3. The jaunty parenthesis, "Hello Everybody," reminds us that we all jaywalk--and that Trippett knows it. It also suggests that he intends his essay to be read by the very typical American scofflaws he deplores.

4. Trippett uses a short, blunt statement of warning as a conclusion. The tone is serious and cautionary, and students may be startled by his departure from an analytical tone. In addition, the disease imagery ("infectiousness," "terminally") heightens the gravity of the situation. The conclusion implies we should act as a society to remedy scofflawry, and so is an example of the conclusion strategy of prediction and recommendation.

ONE VOTE FOR THIS AGE OF ANXIETY

Margaret Mead

Questions for Close Reading (p. 637)

1. Mead's thesis is implied; she argues that anxiety is an indicator of the relative safety of our society (6), and a positive force in motivating people to change and solve problems (13, 16). As she says in paragraph 11, "On balance, our age of anxiety represents a large advance over savage and peasant cultures."

2. Fear results when people are actively threatened with attack, violence, famine, or other disaster (4), while anxiety is the residual and appropriate emotion of modern people who must risk choices and hope for desired results of their efforts. Mead writes, "Anxiety exists as an uneasy state of mind, in which one has a feeling that something unspecified and undeterminable may go wrong" (8). Primitive people fear for their lives, quite literally--enemies, black magic, hunger, volcanoes, bandits, and coups all could destroy them.

3. "Good anxiety," Mead says in paragraph 16, results in an
energetic attempt to solve our society's problems. It is not
just empty worry or regret about the past, but "active, vivid
anxiety about what must be done ... [that] binds men to life
with an intense concern." Such good anxiety is a sign of
hope because it means people will be motivated to "make a
great many more of the right things happen eveywhere..." Such
anxiety prompts us to work for a better future.

4. Discontent comes from worrying about life without a
balancing recognition that life is a "tragedy" where, no
matter what we do or how hard we try, people will always die.
Our seeming lack of connection to death is an illusion. Mead
believes that if we strove to be more in touch with the
reality of death, we would work all the harder to protect
ourselves and our society from the avoidable harms, such as
war and pollution. We might thus become more responsible by
taking appropriate actions.

5. repudiate (1): disapprove of, reject
   castigate (1): criticize severely
   vaunted (1): praised, boasted
   inimical (9): harmful
   transmute (15): change, transform

Questions About the Writer's Craft (p. 637)

1. In several places Mead mentions views she does not agree
with. In her introduction, she discusses the view that
anxiety is a problem of our age; the rest of the essay is a
refutation of this view. Throughout, her mentioning of other
points of view provides a springboard from which to develop her
own idea; such refutation of commonly held ideas is the
foundation of this essay. Other examples of refutation can
be found in paragraph 3, where she mentions the idea that
"savages" live in a simpler, paradisical world lacking in
anxiety, only to refute it by contrasting the fear inherent
in primitive life with modern peoples' vague worries; in
paragraph 13, where she refutes the idea that people's seeing
psychiatrists is a sign of the breakdown of our society; and
in paragraph 17, where she concedes that moderns do have many
life-threatening things to worry about.

2. Mead derides critics of modernity in the first two
paragraphs, using mockery and irony. She exaggerates the
critics' position in order to suggest its absurdity: "When
critics wish torepudiate the world in which we live,
one of their familiarways of doing it is to castigate
modern man because anxietyis his chief problem." Her
disdainful phraseology includes: "our
vaunted progress" (1), "critics and carpers," "do a very
amusingthing," "without much further discussion,
they let us assume..."(2).

3. "Savage" (3, 4) and "peasant" (4, 5) both contain
negative associations. A "savage " suggests an uncivilized,
wild, "cultureless" person; it is ironic that Mead uses this
word because she, as a seminal anthropologist of her time,
promoted the idea that non-Western peoples do have a
culture, just one vastly different from ours. Likewise, the
term "peasant" conveys the image of people helplessly under
the domination of oppressive upper classes. Mead's use of
these terms helps her set off the differences between the
fear of simpler peoples and the anxiety common to moderns.
She uses the terms in an informed way, as someone who has
great knowledge and compassion for the conditions under which
these "primitive" people live. "They are hungry, cold and,

in many parts of the world, they dread that local warfare,
bandits, political coups may endanger their homes, their
meager livelihoods, and their lives" (5), she writes with
great empathy.

4. Many students will not understand the references to the
   killing of Archduke Ferdinand of Austria in the streets of
   Sarajevo, causing young Americans to be drafted to fight in
   World War I, or to Gunnar Myrdal, the prominent Swedish
   sociologist who wrote an important book on race in America in
   the 1950s.   To some extent, these are references that Mead's
   contemporaries in the 1950s would have understood because
   they had, in many cases, lived through the events; she did
   not need to spell out what she meant for this audience.
   Today, however, readers need some education to understand the
   references.

BEAUTY: WHEN THE OTHER DANCER IS THE SELF

Alice Walker

Questions for Close Reading

1. What is the thesis of the selection? Locate the sentence(s) in which Walker states her main idea. If she does not state the thesis explicitly, express it in your own words.

2. Walker mentions two of her brothers by name: Bill in paragraph 32 and Johnny in paragraph 42. Was either of them involved in the shooting incident? What in the essay makes you think so?

3. What is the connection between the loss of young Alice's cat and her teacher's marriage (paragraph 23)?

4. Why, when seeing the desert for the first time (paragraph 44), does Walker remember her doctor's words of so many years before?

5. Refer to your dictionary as needed to define the following words in the selection: subversive (paragraph 1), reputedly (19), abscess (25), valedictorian (32), and cringes (44).

Questions About the Writer's Craft

1. Why does Walker write in the present tense about events that happened long ago?

2. What is the effect of the repeated sentences "I remember," and "'You did not change,' they say"?

3. What does Walker gain by telling her story in a series of short episodes rather than in a more closely connected narrative?

4. Why does Walker make such frequent use of italic type? Does this device add needed emphasis to key words and phrases, or does it occur a little too often to be fully effective?

Questions for Further Thought

1. In paragraphs 12 and 25, Walker tells about the home remedies with which she and her mother were treated. Although she deliberately presents this information without comment, what point is she making about the lives of poor blacks in the region where she grew up?

2. In paragraph 32, Walker reports that after her eye operation she became a different person "almost immediately." Do you think it is common for a person's life to change dramatically overnight?

3. Why does Rebecca's remark, "Mommy, there's a world in your eye," evoke such strong feelings in the author? What, precisely, was she "crying and laughing" about?

4. What does Walker mean by the last paragraph of her essay? What is the image of a person dancing with herself intended to suggest?

Writing Assignments

1. Write an essay about an episode in your life that taught you something important about yourself.

2. Choose another member of your class whom you do not know well. Write a description of that person that relates what you have observed about his or her physical appearance with what you assume he or she is really like. Be sure not to name the person you are describing.

3. Write a series of short autobiographical paragraphs and arrange them in an order that makes a point about how you became the way you are now. Use Walker's essay as a model.

Answers to "Questions for Close Reading"

1. Walker regards growing up as a long process of coming to terms with oneself. Because of her disfiguring injury, she needed to build an image of herself based not upon other people's views of her, but upon values discovered from within. In the end she becomes beautiful because she learns to see the beauty in herself, through acceptance of her own strengths and weaknesses.

2. Bill was probably not one of the brothers involved in the shooting; he is too much older than she to have been playing cowboys and Indians with her when she was a child. Although she does not say so, Johnny was probably the one who shot her. Her questions about the day the incident happened are designed partly to get him to admit he is sorry for having injured her.

3. Both occurred at a time in her life when she felt deserted by everyone--by her parents and grandparents, her favorite teacher, and even her cat.

4. On seeing the desert she realizes for the first time that she has led her life subconsiously expecting to go completely blind at some point.

5. subversive (1): undercutting
   reputedly (19): supposedly
   abscess (25): infection
   valedictorian (32): student who delivers the commence-
                               ment address at graduation
   cringes (47): shrinks back

Answers to "Questions About the Writer's Craft"

1. Using the present tense makes the entire essay more vivid.
   In a sense, all the events are still present in Walker's
   personality--she is implying that their influence persists
   into her adult life.

2. As the sentences are repeated, they gain in force, for the
   reader remembers them from earlier contexts.

3. Walker builds up the story of her life like a mosaic--
   hundreds of bits of tile that together make up a complete
   picture. She is suggesting that a person's life is made
   up of hundreds of separate episodes, all contributing to
   the effect of the whole.

4. Italics add emphasis to important ideas, and they can also
   help to suggest voice patterns, as in paragraph 5. Overdone,
   however, they can become an annoying mannerism as well as
   lose their effectiveness. Walker uses them in this essay
   about as much as they can be used and still be effective.

UNIVERSITY DAYS

James Thurber

Questions for Close Reading

1. What is the thesis of the selection? Locate the sentence(s)
   in which Thurber states his main idea. If he does not state
   the thesis explicitly, express it in your own words.

2. Throughout all of his writings and cartoons, Thurber reveals
   a distaste for authority. Find evidences of this attitude in
   Thurber's descriptions of the authority figures in this essay.

3. From Charlie Chaplin to Woody Allen, humorists have presented
   themselves as loners, different and alienated by that
   difference. How is Thurber different from the rest of the
   college students?

4. As in most television sitcoms, the situations in Thurber's
   essay set up the humor. For example, the university requires
   that everyone--regardless of his or her athletic ability--
   pass swimming. What other situations at Ohio State
   University set up the opportunity for something to go wrong?

5. Refer to your dictionary as needed to define the following
   words in the selection: nebulous (paragraph 1),
   lacteal opacity (4), variegated (4), lanky (13).

Questions About the Writer's Craft

1. Thurber frequently employs sarcasm, or verbal irony, in his
   essay. For example, he says that the "structure of flower
   cells" is "interesting" (paragraph 1). Find other examples
   of sarcasm in which Thurber or another character says the
   opposite of what he really means.

2. Thurber often finds it more effective--and funnier--to use
   dialogue instead of commentary. Find three examples where
   the use of dialogue enhances the humor in the essay.

3. Humorists often rely on stock characters or stereotypes (the
    dumb blonde, the nerdy intellectual, the bratty child). Cite
    Thurber's use of stereotypes, characters who are not three-
    dimensional but merely examples of campus types.

4. Comics take great liberties with exaggeration or hyperbole.
    Find examples of exaggeration that is obvious yet acceptable
    in this humorous framework.

Questions for Further Thought

1. How is the satirist's view a limited one that sees only one
    side of an issue?

2. Thurber takes an absurdist point of view--his college
    experiences become funny because they are ultimately
    meaningless. How is this approach toward life actually a
    survival skill? How can a perception of life's absurd
    events help us survive our everyday dilemmas?

3. At the end of the essay, Thurber comments, "I don't think
    about it much any more." How does the passing of time change
    our perspective on past experiences? When we are older, does
    it become easier to take a humorous view of childhood traumas?

4. Choose a stand-up comic whose style seems closest to
    Thurber's in this essay. Explain the similarities between
    this comic's style and Thurber's.

Writing Assignments

1. Thurber describes the regulations he faced at Ohio State
    University. Write a humorous or serious essay about a set of
    regulations--handed down by parents, church, school, or another
    organization--that you have found harmful or helpful in your
    life.

2. Thurber looked under the surface to disclose some of the
    inadequacies of a college education at Ohio State University.
    Write about an experience you have had that showed how things
    often aren't as perfect as they seem.

3. Write an essay on the difference between satire and other
    forms of humor. How does satire achieve its cutting edge?
    What gives sarcasm its sting? Consider also the popularity
    of satirists such as Robin Williams and Eddie Murphy. Why
    are most modern, stand-up comedians satirists?

Answers to "Questions for Close Reading"

1. Although no thesis statement appears, Thurber's basic premise
    is the absurdity of life in the American university, an
    institution usually associated with higher learning and
    advanced thought.

2. Thurber's botany instructor is constantly "in a fury" and
    even quivers "like Lionel Barrymore." The economics
    professor (paragraphs 5-12) is described as "a thin, timid
    man" who makes train noises in front of his class. In gym,
    the author bumps into "professors," equating them with other
    gym equipment. General Littlefield turns his military
    attention to the swatting of flies (paragraph 18).

3. Thurber is a true loner. He is the only student who can't
   see the cells in botany class. He is uncomfortable
   "stripped" in gym class and cannot swim across the pool
   (paragraph 13). Just as he draws his own eye to annoy
   the botany instructor, Thurber is always the removed
   observer--the outsider.

4. Many situations lay the grounds for humor in this essay.
   Universities that admit students on the basis of athletic
   ability, like the football hero in economics, place the
   weaker student in impossible academic situations. The school
   newspaper has a "beat" reporter who cannot find letters on a
   typewriter. Treating young students in a military fashion is
   also begging for trouble, because they lack the discipline.
   Thurber employs all of these situations to humorous effect.

5. nebulous (1): cloudy, hazy, vague
   lacteal opacity (4): milky
   variegated (4): having streaks, marks or patches of
                   color
   lanky (13): tall, thin

Answers to "Questions About the Writer's Craft"

1. Thurber's basic tone is sarcastic, and the essay is
   replete with examples. When Thurber says that the football
   player "was not dumber than an ox" but "not any smarter," he
   simply means that Bolenciecwcz is an idiot (and can he spell
   his own name?!). When the author says that one agricultural
   student took up journalism to "fall back on newspaper work"
   if farming fails, he really means that the student is too
   incompetent even to be a journalist.

2. When Thurber draws his own reflected eye for the botany
   teacher, the instructor's response ("You didn't, you didn't,
   you didn't!") is much funnier than a statement such as, "He
   couldn't believe it" (4). The dialogue between Mr. Bassum
   and Bolenciecwcz (5-12) speaks for itself. And having
   General Littlefield shout, "That man is the only man who has
   it right!" is much funnier than Thurber simply saying he was
   the only one who had it right.

3. Bolenciecwcz is the classic dumb football player--a Southern
   accent is even thrown in to add insult to injury. Thurber
   himself comes off as a classic nerd in glasses, lacking in
   athletic ability and incompetent as a soldier. General
   Littlefield is the typical military lifer; he doesn't
   speak--he "shouts," "barks" and "snaps." The farmer/
   journalist represents the classic hayseed; like his stories,
   he is "dull and colorless." And Professor Bassum is the
   stereotyped, "thin" little academic.

4. Exaggeration is rampant in this story. It is unlikely that
   any professor would make quite as many transportation
   examples of onomatopeia ("Choo-choo," "Chuffa chuffa").
   Thurber also stretches his limits when he is the only squad
   member to get the drill right--and then to be made corporal!
   The behavior of the botany instructor borders on a nervous
   breakdown. Still, Thurber gets away with all of this
   exaggeration through his innate skill as a humorist. The
   author reveals the importance of stretching a point for comic
   effect.

A MODEST PROPOSAL

Jonathan Swift

Questions for Close Reading

1. What is the thesis of the selection? Locate the sentence(s) in which Swift states his main idea. If he does not state the thesis explicitly, express it in your own words.

2. At what point in the essay does the reader realize that Swift's "modest proposal" is cannibalism?

3. Why will Swift's proposal provoke no objection in England? What is the real point of this argument?

4. What is Swift's real attitude to the alternative remedies listed in paragraph 29 for the depressed state of Ireland?

5. Refer to your dictionary as needed to define the following words in the selection: prodigious (paragraph 2), raiment (4), rudiments (6), encumbrance (19), and inclemencies (32).

Questions About the Writer's Craft

1. Swift's "modest" proposal is in fact so monstrous that even some people who recognize its satirical intention are appalled and disgusted by it. Do you think Swift is justified in resorting to such drastic means to make his point?

2. In paragraph 23, Swift refers to a one-year-old child as a "yearling," a term ordinarily used only of animals. In what other ways does Swift draw a parallel between children and livestock?

3. Jonathan Swift never married, nor did he have any children. Why does he say in paragraph 33 that his wife is past childbearing and his youngest child is nine years old?

4. Reread paragraph 4. Did you realize, as you read the essay the first time, that this lengthy paragraph consists of only two sentences? What methods does Swift use to keep his readers from getting lost in his long, involved sentences?

Questions for Further Thought

1. Is satire still an effective method for influencing social and political attitudes? Think of examples of modern-day satire and discuss how seriously people take the ideas they express.

2. Much modern day satire is humorous. Do you think "A Modest Proposal" contains much humor, or is the subject matter too grim even to provoke a smile?

3. Jonathan Swift's epitaph in St. Patrick's Cathedral in Dublin says, "He has gone where savage indignation can no longer lacerate his heart." Do you think "A Modest Proposal" reflects the "savage indignation" mentioned in the epitaph?

4. What injustices do you see in modern society that might inspire another "proposal" from Swift if he were alive today?

Writing Assignments

1. Write an essay describing your attitude toward people who are much poorer or richer than you are.

2. Try to imitate some of Swift's more complicated sentences by writing sentences of your own that follow the same general pattern. After some practice, try writing a paragraph such as 17 or 18, choosing your own subject matter but using the same number of sentences of approximately the same length as Swift's.

3. Try your hand at writing a satire. Choose a subject close to home, such as a situation in your own school or town, that you think deserves to be exposed as wrong-headed or ridiculous. Remember: most satire is not as harsh as Swift's; it should be possible to make your point without being hurtful or vulgar.

Answers to "Questions for Close Reading"

1. Swift is exposing the extent to which the rich were exploiting the poor in the Ireland of his time. He suggests that because the rich are already devouring the poor in a figurative sense, they might as well take the next logical step and eat them—literally. His technique is called reductio ad absurdum, which means carrying an idea to its logical conclusion in order to reveal its underlying absurdity.

2. The proposal itself is first stated in paragraph 9.

3. He says in paragraph 31 that since human flesh is too delicate to export, "we incur no danger in disobliging England." The point is that the English government cares nothing about what happens in Ireland unless it threatens to damage English trade.

4. He thinks that they have little or no chance of being carried out.

5. prodigious (2): enormous
   raiment (4): garment
   rudiments (6): basics
   encumbrance (19): handicap
   inclemencies (32): severities

Answers to "Questions About the Writer's Craft"

1. This must always remain a matter of opinion. However, the bitterness of Swift's satire reflects the appalling conditions he saw around him every day.

2. In paragraph 24 he refers to mothers as "breeders," and in paragraph 26 he says that if his proposal were taken up, men would attach as much value to their wives as they do to their cows and sows.

3. Swift is speaking not in his own person but through a character invented for the purpose, a solid, unimaginative citizen who has only his country's good at heart. This character talks about his own family situation to prove he has no personal interest in seeing his proposal adopted— another brilliant satiric touch.

4. Although Swift's sentences are sometimes enormously long, they seldom backtrack. Each clause carries the thought further, almost as though it were a separate sentence. Long sentences become difficult to read only when the reader must carry an early portion of the sentence in his mind in order to connect it with an element that occurs towards the end.

WHERE DO WE GO FROM HERE: COMMUNITY OR CHAOS?

Martin Luther King, Jr.

Questions for Close Reading

1. What is the thesis of the selection? Locate the sentence(s) in which King states his main idea. If he does not state the thesis explicitly, express it in your own words.

2. What was King's attitude toward U. S. involvement in the Vietnam War? What is your evidence for this?

3. What evidence does King provide to support his belief that war is obsolete?

4. What step does King believe is necessary before people can solve the complex problems of achieving disarmament and peace?

5. Refer to your dictionary as needed to define the following words in the selection: proliferation (paragraph 1), brigands (4), precipitate (7), calamitous (9), and inexorably (9).

Questions About the Writer's Craft

1. How would you describe King's tone throughout this essay? What words can you find that help establish this tone?

2. What is King's purpose in paragraph 2? Why do you suppose he made this particular point at the beginning of the essay?

3. King cites an irony of history in paragraph 5, remarking that Hitler could pursue a nakedly aggressive expansionist policy in the name of peace. Does King himself use verbal irony to make his point?

4. Martin Luther King was more famous as a public speaker and as a preacher than as a writer. Find examples in the essay of language that would be appropriate for a speech or a sermon.

Questions for Further Thought

1. In paragraph 5, King refers to Adolf Hitler as a "megalomaniac." Are there national leaders on the world stage today who could properly be described as megalomaniacs? Look up the word in a dictionary to make certain you understand its precise meaning.

2. King calls the United Nations "a gesture in the direction of nonviolence" in paragraph 12. What changes in the way the UN functions does King suggest? Do you think his suggestions would work in practice?

3. King argues in paragraph 10 that nonviolence should become "a subject for study and serious experimentation in every field of human conflict." Choose three areas of human conflict and suggest a possible experiment in nonviolence appropriate to each.

4. King says he does not minimize the complexity of the problems that need to be solved before peace can be achieved. What do you think are the real barriers to peace?

Writing Assignments

1. Imagine that a child has asked you to explain a violent action he or she has seen on television or in real life. Write an essay in simple language explaining how violence occurs and how you think we should feel about it.

2. Write an essay about a situation in your life that might have led to violence but didn't. How was violence avoided? Do you regard that episode as a model for solving future problems without resorting to physical conflict?

3. Write a letter to a public official explaining your views on disarmament and world peace.

Answers to "Questions for Close Reading"

1. In paragraph 8, King says, "We must pursue peaceful ends through peaceful means." In paragraph 15, he concludes, "We must shift the arms race into a 'peace race.'"

2. King opposed the Vietnam war. He states his position on it in paragraph 6.

3. He shows that, because of the enormous power of modern weapons, even a just war would be far too destructive to accomplish its ends.

4. King believes that a "mental and spiritual re-evaluation" must take place so that mankind may find "the will, the courage and the insight" to achieve peace on earth (paragraph 13).

5. proliferation (1): spread
   brigands (4): thugs, criminals
   precipitate (5): hasten
   calamitous (9): disastrous
   inexorably (9): relentlessly

Answers to "Questions About the Writer's Craft"

1. King's tone is serious and urgent throughout. Phrases such as "highways of death" (paragraph 9) and "a calamitous legacy of human suffering" (9) help convey the importance and gravity of the issues he is addressing.

2. His purpose in paragraph 2 is to show how useless war is. He is showing at the outset that man is capable of achieving anything he sets his mind to--even peace.

3. In paragraph 4 he speaks of the military advisors who surround world leaders as "bands of brigands each bearing unsheathed swords."

4. Some of King's written sentences build to the kind of climax
    that is very effective in public speaking. The first
    sentence of paragraph 2 is a good example. Rhetorical
    questions ("Do we have the morality and the courage. . .?")
    are also very popular with public speakers.

IN BED

Joan Didion

Questions for Close Reading

1. What is the thesis of the selection? Locate the sentence(s)
    in which Didion states her main idea. If she does not state
    the thesis explicitly, express it in your own words.

2. Didion points out that others' attitudes about her migraines
    have been less than understanding. Find three points in the
    essay where the author seems defensive about her condition.

3. Why would "lost laundry" or "canceled appointments"--and
    not the loss of her husband or open warfare in the
    streets--result in a headache for the author (paragraph 7)?

4. Didion relates that the "migraine personality. . .tends to be
    ambitious, inward, intolerant of error, rigidly organized,
    perfectionist" (paragraph 6). Find examples from the essay
    that reveal any of these traits in the author.

5. Refer to your dictionary as needed to define the following
    words in the selection: circumnavigation (paragraph 1),
    contretemps (3), predisposition (3),
    contraindications (4), and aphasia (5).

Questions About the Writer's Craft

1. Transitions serve as one of the professional writer's most
    useful tools. The repetition of a word (or words) in the last
    sentence of one paragraph and the first sentence of the next
    is a well-known transitional device. Locate three examples
    of repetitional transitions and comment on Didion's use
    of them.

2. Imagery is the use of language to convey sense
    experiences (taste, touch, sound, smell, sight). For example,
    "ice" (paragraph 2) conjures up images of taste and touch.
    Find other words in the essay that convey strong sense
    experiences.

3. Explain the use of "the wind. . .coming up" (paragraph 7)
    as an example of figurative language, specifically,
    symbolism. How does the increasing wind function on
    both a literal and a symbolic level?

4. The list is an important device for Didion, who uses this
    writing tool specifically for emphasis. Find three lists in
    which the examples convey perfectly the author's point.

Questions for Further Thought

1. Once Didion learned to stop fighting her migraines, she learned to overcome them. In life's difficult times, when is it better simply to "lie down and let it happen" (paragraph 8)? When should we keep on fighting?

2. The writer Ernest Hemingway once noted that "everyone breaks, but most are stronger in the broken places." How has Didion's debilitating condition made her stronger? What "breaking" experiences have actually strengthened you in the long run?

3. Do most people pay a high price for perfectionism? What are some of the modern health problems that can be attributed to compulsive behavior?

4. Many writers have pointed out the importance of contraries in our life. Could we have pleasure without pain? What purpose does pain serve in our everyday lives?

Writing Assignments

1. The author learned how to live with what could have been a debilitating illness. Tell how you or someone you know has conquered a potentially crippling problem.

2. Didion graphically describes a migraine so that you, her readers, can tell the difference between it and an ordinary headache. Describe something physical that you have experienced to allow your readers a similar insight.

3. Write a descriptive essay about something negative. Try to apply some of Didion's writing techniques: the use of lists, repetitional transitions, and so on. By the end of the essay, struggle to turn your negative subject into a positive one.

Answers to "Questions for Close Reading"

1. Most students should cite "We have reached a certain understanding, my migraine and I" (paragraph 7) as the thesis statement. The preceding sentence, "And I have learned now to live with it, learned when to expect it, etc.," also illustrates the controlling idea of Didion's essay. Students may state, in their own words, that the writer attempts to show how people can overcome a certain problem while educating the reader in the process. Basically, Didion writes the essay to show she has made peace with her suffering.

2. Most of Didion's tone is defensive, so that examples abound. When she says, ". . . as everyone who didn't have them knew," she is defensive (paragraph 2). Other examples include: "I spent yesterday in bed with a headache not merely because of my bad attitude. . ." (3), ". . . the accusing eye of someone who has never had a headache" (6), and "this common conviction that we are perversely refusing to cure ourselves by taking a couple of aspirin" (6).

3. The laundry and appointments hit close to home. They function as symbols of the everyday disappointments that take their toll on all of us--and take a special toll on migraine sufferers.

4. The writer admits that she is a "perfectionist" about her writing (paragraph 6). She is "intolerant of error" in herself, as she struggles to hide her problem at all cost--even with "involuntary tears" running down her face (2). To overcome her problem she even concentrates on her pain (8), a sign of an "inward" personality.

5. circumnavigation (1): sailing around
   contretemps (3): mishap, embarrassing occurrence
   predisposition (3): tendency, inclination
   contraindications (4): warnings
   aphasia (5): inability to articulate ideas

Answers to "Questions About the Writer's Craft"

1. The following words repeat and connect thoughts between paragraphs: "migraine" (last sentence in paragraph 5, first sentence in paragraph 6), "perfectionism, perfectionist" (6,7), "comes" (7,8). Students should see how this device aids in the transition of thoughts between paragraphs.

2. Students should see that specific words like "needle" (7) carry more imagery than abstract words like "pain." Other imagery-laden words include: "laundry" (sight, smell), "aspirin" (touch, taste) and "red lights" (sight).

3. The imminent arrival of the wind (7) symbolizes the arrival of another migraine--it blows in unexpectedly. The wind is blowing, literally, but it functions as a symbol of the writer's inability to stop the arrival of her headache.

4. The lists bring home the author's experiences. While still fighting her condition (paragraph 2), the author "went to school. . .sat through lectures. . .threw up in washrooms, stumbled home by instinct, emptied ice trays. . . ." The list emphasizes the complexity of fighting such a problem. The range of catalysts for a migraine includes: "stress, allergy, fatigue, an abrupt change in barometric pressure, a contretemps over a parking ticket" (3). A number of other lists occur as well (paragraphs 5, 6 and 7).